Blaise Pascal

Twayne's World Authors Series

French Literature

Maxwell A. Smith, Editor

Guerry Professor of French, Emeritus
The University of Chattanooga
Former Visiting Professor in Modern Languages
The Florida State University

TWAS 701

t by Quesnel
naux

Blaise Pascal

By Hugh M. Davidson

University of Virginia

Twayne Publishers • *Boston*

Blaise Pascal

Hugh M. Davidson

Copyright © 1983 by G. K. Hall & Company
All Rights Reserved
Published by Twayne Publishers
A Division of G. K. Hall & Company
70 Lincoln Street
Boston, Massachusetts 02111

Book Production by Marne B. Sultz

Book Design by Barbara Anderson

Printed on permanent/durable acid-free
paper and bound in the United States of
America.

Library of Congress Cataloging in Publication Data

Davidson, Hugh McCullough, 1918–
    Blaise Pascal.

    (Twayne's world authors series ; TWAS 701)
    Bibliography: p. 142
    Includes index.
    1. Pascal, Blaise, 1623–1662. I. Title. II. Series.
B1903.D35   1983   230'.2   83–8438
ISBN 0–8057–6548–4

11/6/13

4/78

To L. and A.

330.3
P378

Contents

About the Author

Hugh M. Davidson is Commonwealth Professor of French literature at the University of Virginia. He received the A.B. and Ph.D. degrees from the University of Chicago. Before going to Virginia in 1973 he taught at the University of Chicago, Dartmouth College, and the Ohio State University. In 1979–80 he was Thomas Jefferson Fellow of Downing College, Cambridge, and in 1982–83 visiting professor at the University of Paris (Sorbonne). He is at present working on two sets of studies: one on the concept of literary art in France in the seventeenth century, and the other on Pascal's distinctive habits of thought and language.

Preface

This introduction to Pascal surveys his achievement as a mathematician, as a physicist, and above all as a moralist deeply engaged in theological questions. It also provides guidance for those who wish to read Pascal and to develop their own understanding of his thought. To this end it stresses important themes and ways of thinking that recur in the works; it defines problems and attempts to say, in a short book, how Pascal goes about solving those problems. As a survey it gives a report of Pascal's views and conclusions; as a guide to his main concerns it will, I hope, enable the curious reader to see something of what Pascal sees and to rethink the issues with him. To learn about Pascal is valuable, of course; to learn with him is a particularly exciting and satisfying experience, quite apart from whether one finally accepts his way of stating and answering the great questions that hold his attention.

The account presented in chapter 1 follows the main strands in Pascal's life, noting the milieus, the personal relationships, and the intellectual and moral interests that emerge in its various stages. The next three chapters take up those interests in a more detailed way. In chapter 2 the investigations and discoveries of Pascal in mathematics and physics are treated untechnically but in a way that shows their essential aspects. In chapter 3, the *Provinciales* make the transition from arithmetic, geometry, and physics to another kind of truth—religious belief, based on authority and revelation rather than on reasoning and sense experience. Chapter 4 analyzes the *Pensées*, which draw together for us the moral and religious—even mystical, by moments—tendencies that come to predominate in Pascal's mind; it is a monumental accomplishment in spite of being in fact a collection of fragments. In chapter 5 an effort is made to define the unity of Pascal's thought, not by putting everything into a single, tightly integrated vision (I doubt that that can be done), but by bringing together distinct approaches to the truth about nature, man, and God that at the last complement each other and have the unity of an ensemble. Chapter 6 relates Pascal and his interests to what some of his contemporaries were doing, and then, since he has never ceased to be an active presence on the intellectual scene in France and elsewhere, reports on what some eminent readers have seen in him and said about him in the last three centuries.

The *opuscules* or shorter works of Pascal could not be the subject of a detailed study here. But they are not insignificant, nor are they irrelevant to the two aims I have set for myself. In chapter 7 I have summarized them and indicated how one may establish thematic ties and other relationships between them and the *Provinciales* and the *Pensées*. The contents of this chapter may be especially useful for readers dependent on translations, since these shorter pieces are less available in English versions than the two works for which Pascal is best known.

I wish to thank Professor Maxwell A. Smith for his suggestions and patience as I have gone about preparing this *Pascal* for the Twayne World Authors Series, and also the colleagues and friends at Downing College, Cambridge, who during the Michaelmas term of 1979 offered me pleasant surroundings in which to complete it.

Thanks are also due to the many *pascalisants* from whose work I have drawn freely; without them I would not have attempted a work of this scope. I must mention in particular M. Jean Mesnard of the Sorbonne whose fruitful labors have helped immensely all those who study Pascal's life and works.

Hugh M. Davidson

University of Virginia

Chronology

1623   19 June, Blaise Pascal born at Clermont in Auvergne, the son of Etienne and Antoinette (Begon) Pascal.

1626   Death of Pascal's mother.

1631   Etienne Pascal leaves Clermont, establishes himself and family in Paris.

1635–1636   Blaise's first contacts with the Académie Mersenne, a group of Parisian mathematicians to which Etienne Pascal belonged.

1640   "Essai pour les coniques," the sketch of a treatise on conic sections. Family moves to Rouen.

1642–1643   Pascal invents the *machine arithmétique* or arithmetical machine, a device for carrying out computations mechanically.

1646   Pascal family, strongly touched by Jansenist piety, is "converted" to a more fervent religious life. First experiments by Pascal in connection with the problem of the *vide* or vacuum.

1647   Pascal in poor health; returns to Paris with Jacqueline. Exchanges ideas with Descartes on the subject of the vacuum. Experiments on it are published as *Expériences nouvelles touchant le vide* [New experiments concerning the vacuum]; controversy with Père Noël. Contacts with the convent of Port-Royal in Paris, the center of Jansenist spirituality.

1648   19 September, experiment conceived by Pascal to test his theory of the vacuum successfully carried out by his brother-in-law.

1651   Pascal prepares a treatise on the vacuum (that remained unfinished); important preface. 24 September, Pascal's father dies.

1652   Pascal sends a *machine arithmétique* to Queen Christina of Sweden, and with it a substantial letter.

1653   Pascal in the entourage of the duc de Roannez; becomes acquainted with the Chevalier de Méré and the financier Damien Mitton.

1654 Finishes treatise on the equilibrium of liquids and on the weight of the atmosphere. Conversations with Méré, correspondence with Fermat lead to research on the calculus of probabilities. Preparation of the treatise on the arithmetical triangle. 23 November, undergoes an intense religious experience, recorded in the *Mémorial*, resulting in a decisive commitment (the so-called "second conversion").

1655 Retreat at Port-Royal for three weeks; probable date of the reflections reported in Fontaine's *Entretien avec M. de Saci* [Conversation with M. de Saci]. Probable date at year's end and early in 1656, of the *Ecrits sur la grâce* [Writings on grace].

1656 23 January, beginning of series of *Provinciales* [Provincial (letters)] in defense of Arnauld and Port-Royal; published intermittently until May of 1657 (eighteen letters in all). 24 March, the miracle of the Holy Thorn: the cure of Pascal's niece, Marguerite Périer. Pascal's reflections on miracles inspire the project of an apology or defense of the Christian religion; during the next two years he prepares notes on the subject.

1658 11 June, date of the *Cinquième écrit des curés de Paris* [Fifth writing by the priests of Paris], a text written against the Jesuits. Discoveries concerning the cycloid curve ("la roulette") and its properties; the international contest and its unsatisfactory ending.

1659 February, Pascal seriously ill, incapable of sustained intellectual activity for more than a year. The period of the "Prière pour demander à Dieu le bon usage des maladies" [Prayer asking God for the right use of illnesses].

1660 Pascal in Clermont with the Périer family. Indications of continuing work on the apology. Notes made for the "Discourses on the condition of men of high rank."

1661 Renewal of controversy over the doctrines of Jansenius;

upheaval at Port-Royal. Pascal, at odds with Arnauld and Nicole, withdraws from further contention.

1662   Opening, in March, of the first omnibus carriage route in Paris, an invention of Pascal and the duc de Roannez. June, Pascal in very poor health, lives with his sister, Gilberte. 19 August, Pascal dies; burial in the church of Saint-Etienne-du-Mont.

1663   Publication of the treatises on the equilibrium of liquids and on the weight of the atmosphere.

1665   Publication of the treatise on the arithmetical triangle.

1670   Publication of selected and edited items from Pascal's papers in a collection entitled *Pensées de M. Pascal sur la religion et sur quelques autres sujets* [Thoughts of M. Pascal on religion and on some other subjects]—the first edition of the *Pensées*.

Chapter One

The Life of Pascal

Beginnings (1623–31)

Blaise Pascal was born on 19 June 1623 in the provincial town of Clermont en Auvergne, now Clermont-Ferrand. At the time France was on the upswing of a new cultural movement. After the weak regency of Marie de Medicis, Louis XIII took up again the work of pacification and reconstruction that Henri IV had begun. He sought to repair the damage done in France by the religious wars of the sixteenth century. In 1624 Richelieu became the king's principal minister, and until his death in 1642 he prepared the way for the royal absolutism that was to come with Louis XIV. The first three decades of the seventeenth century saw the rise of several new conceptions: of poetry with Malherbe, of drama with Corneille, of philosophy with Descartes, of manners and speech with salons such as that of Mme de Rambouillet. To this movement, particularly clear to us in historical hindsight but recognized also while it was occurring, Pascal was to make a unique contribution.

His mother, Antoinette Begon, was the daughter of a merchant in Clermont. His father, Etienne Pascal, belonged to the *petite noblesse*, to the class of what we would call civil servants. Martin Pascal, the father of Etienne and the grandfather of Blaise, had been engaged in tax gathering; he had at one time the impressive title of king's counselor, treasurer of France, and general of royal finances in the district of Riom (which included Clermont). Etienne Pascal went away to Paris for his law studies. On his return to Clermont in 1610, he bought the post of *conseiller élu du roi*, which made him a judge in the lower tax court. His fortunes prospering, he became finally *second président* of the *Cour des aides*, the court of final judgment in matters having to do with taxes and duties in the region. Both in Clermont and in the province he was a prominent member of an elite composed of the upper bourgeoisie and the *noblesse de robe* (a class of nobility whose rank was conferred for offices held). As he

had something of the sixteenth-century humanist in his temperament
and training, he was no doubt already cultivating his interests in
classical languages, mathematics, and the sciences of nature (then
conceived to be a part of philosophy).

Pascal's mother died in 1626, when he was three years old. He
had two sisters, one older and one younger than he: Gilberte, born
in 1620, and Jacqueline, born in 1625. Etienne Pascal never remar-
ried, and the story of the family became that of profound but changing relationships within this closely knit group. There is little that is
certain to tell about the childhood of Blaise. But in her *Vie de M.
Pascal* [Life of M. Pascal] written apparently soon after her brother's
death in 1662, Gilberte makes clear that from the first he showed
signs of precociousness.

Dès que mon frère fut en âge qu'on lui pût parler il donna des marques
d'un esprit tout extraordinaire par les petites réponses qu'il faisait fort à
propos, mais encore plus par les questions sur la nature des choses qui
surprenaient tout le monde. Ce commencement ne se démentit jamais, car
à mesure qu'il croissait en âge, il augmentait en force de raisonnement,
de sorte qu'il était beaucoup au-dessus de ses forces.[1]

She recalls also her father's great affection for his only son, and the
fact that he could not resign himself to leaving the education of
Blaise to some third person or persons. And so in 1631 at the age of
forty-three, wealthy, imperious, self-confident, Etienne Pascal decided
to sell to his brother (also named Blaise) his post as *Président en
la cour des Aides* and to move to Paris. There he could administer
his fortune, pursue his intellectual interests, and educate his children.

Paris: 1631–39

The period from the establishment of the family in Paris to the
beginning of Etienne Pascal's mission to Normandy and the stay in
Rouen was significant and formative in many ways. To manage the
household and to be a governess for the children, Etienne engaged
Louise Delfaut, of the petite bourgeoisie with origins in Coulommiers.
She remained faithfully with the Pascal family for twenty years and
still had ties with them at the time of her death in 1658. But the
father did not turn the children entirely over to her or to anyone
else; he had a plan and way of instruction that he evidently con-

sidered better than anything available in the convents and *collèges* of Paris. It seems to have worked with his three children; it no doubt contributed much to the unusually intelligent and responsible attitude of Gilberte, and it provided the stimulus for the development of Blaise and Jacqueline, whose special talents were obvious. For one thing, Etienne Pascal appears to have made the most of object lessons, of little introductions to precise knowledge that could be tied to everyday things and happenings—such, for example, as a theory of sound taught in connection with the noises made by cutlery against different kinds of dishes. He had also a distinctive approach to training in languages. He encouraged the children to reason things out, to rely not so much on memory as on some insight into linguistic principles.

The father's intended plan for Blaise was to go through language studies first and then to introduce mathematics. But this restriction, in accord with a law that seems to operate almost without fail in such cases, served only to whet Pascal's curiosity about mathematics and—especially—geometry. His father thought to satisfy him with the statement that geometry studies precisely-drawn figures and the relations one may establish among them. Pascal took this as a point of departure and, working on his own with figures drawn on the floor of the room where he played, began to think along truly geometrical lines in terms of definitions and axioms. When asked one day by his father what he was doing, he indicated that he was trying to express the relationship between the angles of a triangle and two right angles—that is, he was working on what is the thirty-second proposition in book 1 of Euclid's *Elements of Geometry*. It is not true, as some have said, that he had reinvented the theorems of Euclid to that point. Still, it was an astonishing performance; and it seemed so marvelous to his father that he no longer sought to hold Blaise back in the study of mathematics.

His leading pedagogical principle, according to Gilberte, was always to keep the child above his work, "tenir cet enfant au-dessus de son ouvrage." Here we have, perhaps, the origin of something very characteristic of Pascal's later work, his habit of abstract reflection—over and above the niceties of solutions—on problems as such, on how to pose them properly and how to treat them methodically.

And so Etienne Pascal changed the order of studies he had intended to follow. Without neglecting languages and other subjects, he took up at once the mathematical and scientific education of

Blaise. No conflict with religious beliefs or practice was ever felt: as Gilberte says of her father, he held as a principle that the realm of faith is entirely distinct from that of reason, with corresponding differences in subject matters (in her words, "que tout ce qui est l'objet de la foi ne le saurait être de la raison").[2] This way of thinking, which resembles the distinction of "ordres" that Pascal was to elaborate in the *Provinciales* and in the *Pensées* left father and son free to cultivate their scientific interests.

They soon took their place in one of the centers of French and European intellectual life. Marin Mersenne, of the religious order of the *Minimes*, and referred to universally as "le Père Mersenne," founded in 1635 an *académie* composed of a group of people curious about mathematics, physics, and astronomy, and Etienne Pascal was one of the first members. He and Blaise came therefore into personal contact with Mersenne, Roberval, Desargues, Mydorge, and, by correspondence, with Descartes, Fermat, and others. Mersenne's academy was in fact a point of convergence and diffusion of scientific knowledge and advances. Blaise had the opportunity to hear the proceedings and to participate in them. At the age of sixteen he was preparing a "Traité des coniques," one fragment (or résumé) of which was published in 1640 with the title, "Essai pour les coniques." This one-page document, which we shall discuss later, defines conic sections and then indicates a way of deducing their properties from one essential theorem. Although some ideas of Desargues served as inspiration for it (Pascal acknowledged that fact), the "essai" was much praised at the time.

The social life of the family went beyond the circle of scientific friends. At first it appears that the Pascals saw mainly people from their native region who visited Paris or had established themselves there. But their acquaintance widened as time passed. Jacques Le Pailleur was a close friend of the family, his ties going back, perhaps, to Etienne's student days in Paris. A good mathematician, he was also a *bon vivant* with literary tastes who knew the poets Benserade, Saint-Amant, and Dalibray. This last, who came to know the Pascal family well, lived with his widowed sister, Mme de Sainctot. She had been a friend of Voiture, "l'âme du rond" ("the soul of the circle of friends") at the Hôtel de Rambouillet, and had, indeed, a salon of her own. Her two daughters and the Pascal children played together. Later the Pascals came to know the Barillon family, important in legal circles, the future duc de Roannez, and his sister Charlotte.

In this company, at least, Jacqueline Pascal was perhaps more widely known than her brother. She wrote light poetry—stanzas, sonnets, dizains, quatrains, impromptus, epigrams—and she once collaborated with the daughters of Mme de Sainctot in composing a play in verse, which they performed before a large company. When she was thirteen (in 1638), she wrote some verses on the pregnancy of the queen, a feat that led to her being presented to Anne d'Autriche.

Actually this occasion formed an episode in a story that showed how quickly fortunes could change under Richelieu. Early in 1638 the government needed money to pay its armies engaged in what we know as the Thirty Years' War. The royal treasury being depleted, taxes were raised and dividends on investments were cut or not paid. Etienne Pascal saw his situation worsening suddenly and he went, with about four hundred other protesting investors, to the Hôtel de Ville. There were some threats and a few acts of violence. Richelieu reacted promptly: he had the leaders put in the Bastille. Etienne Pascal was obliged to hide in order to avoid that fate, and then to take refuge back in Clermont. A year elapsed before he could reappear safely in Paris, where the children had remained. Jacqueline Pascal and her muse cooperated in the efforts being made by friends of the family to smooth over the affair. It was during this time that she composed not only the verses celebrating the *grossesse* of the queen, but also and later a short work on "the movement that the queen felt from her [unborn] child," thus giving poetic recognition to what must have been the first public act of Louis XIV.[3] But nothing happened in the way of a pardon for her father.

In November of 1638 Jacqueline had smallpox, and Etienne Pascal came back to Paris in secret to take care of her. She recovered, though her face was badly disfigured. Then, in February of the next year, the duchesse d'Aiguillon, who was the niece of Richelieu, recruited her among other children to take part in a play to be given before Richelieu himself. Jacqueline played the part of Cassandra in *L'Amour tyrannique* [Tyrannical love] of Scudéry. After the performance, when she was received by Richelieu, "la petite Pascal" read him a compliment in verse that included a request that her father be allowed to return from exile. She got her wish, and Richelieu asked that the father and his three children pay him a visit. This Etienne Pascal hastened to do at Rueil, where the cardinal happened to be. Jacqueline read an epigram written for the occasion; Richelieu greeted the father and congratulated him on his family; and all was well.

A few months later, at the end of that year, Richelieu apparently decided he could count on the experience and loyalty of Etienne Pascal. He named him "Commissaire député de sa Majesté" to upper Normandy with the task of setting and collecting taxes, reinstalling him thus in functions with which the Pascal family had been associated for a long time and from which at least part of its fortunes had been made. The appointment required a move to Rouen.

Turning Points (Rouen: 1639–47)

The nine years during which the family was based in Rouen proved to be decisive in several ways: in the furtherance of Etienne Pascal's career and position, in religious belief and devotion, and in scientific inquiries.

For various reasons, including poverty and an epidemic of the plague, the population of Normandy was in a state of near rebellion. Richelieu intended to regain control of the situation by a judicious use of force and administrative talent. A bloody repression in January of 1640 showed that he meant business; then in the months that followed the affairs of the province were put in better order, especially in the fixing and gathering of taxes. These matters were Etienne Pascal's specialty, and he acquitted himself so well that in 1645 he received the honor and title of "Conseiller d'Etat." The social life of the family continued along the lines already noticeable in Clermont and in Paris: it was linked to the milieu of magistrates and other officials; and it included, as before, cultivation of literary and intellectual tastes. Corneille became a friend of the family. He took an interest in Jacqueline's poetry, which as time passed gained in vigor and was less marked by signs of effort and naive *préciosité.*

Etienne Pascal had many long and tiring calculations to make in keeping his accounts in order. Blaise was enlisted to help him here as in other aspects of his work. After a while Pascal saw the possibility of lightening the task by an ingenious application of things he knew from geometry and mechanics. He arrived at the idea of a machine consisting of wheels and gears so adjusted that the four basic operations of arithmetic could be performed on it. But executing the idea was difficult: it took two years—beginning in 1642—of trials and reworkings with different materials and artisans to bring the device to the point of being reliable, portable, and durable. The "Pascale" or "Pascaline," as the machine was called, attracted a great deal of attention. Among many others, Mersenne, Roberval, and Huyghens complimented the young inventor; Dalibray wrote a sonnet in his honor; Bourdelot invited him in 1644 to give a demonstration of it to the prince de Condé. Séguier granted Pascal a *privilège*—something like a patent—so that the machine would be protected from counterfeiting. For Pascal not only savored the fame his machine brought him; he clearly intended to make and sell it as a commercial venture. However, because it was difficult and expensive to manufacture, the plan was abandoned, and the *machine arithmétique* remained a much-admired curiosity.

Two important changes occurred in the family. In 1641 Gilberte, the oldest child (she was then twenty-one years old) married her cousin, Florin Périer, and moved back to Clermont, where he was establishing himself. The second change was less external: it concerned the evolution of the family's attitude toward religion, as a result of contact with Jansenism.

Etienne Pascal slipped and fell on ice in January of 1646, injuring his hip. He asked two brothers, the "frères Deschamps" to treat him. After undergoing a religious conversion, they had some medical training and then devoted themselves to works of charity and healing. In their way they reflected the intensification of interest in religion that was taking place in Rouen. They took their particular line of thought from the writings of the Abbé de Saint-Cyran (1581–1643), who had expounded the ideas of Jansenius in France and had been an influential spiritual guide at Port-Royal. They stayed in the Pascal household for three months, a period that gave them the opportunity to do some missionary work. Their example, the books they read, the views they held all greatly affected Blaise (then twenty-three years old).

He experienced at this time what is usually called his "first conversion." The phrase does not mean what one might think at first glance. The Pascals were Christians already, so there was no question of their going from unbelief to belief. "Conversion," as used by Saint-Cyran, referred to a renewal and deepening of religious conviction and practice. The heart, as seat of desire and volition, could be attached to God or to the world; there was no escaping that alternative; and Saint-Cyran and his followers presented it in the clearest possible

light. Since most Christians led in fact lives at least partly governed
by worldly interests, they needed to face the choice squarely and to
reorient themselves wholeheartedly. That is the sense of "conversion"
here, and along with it went the notion of commitment (*vocation*)
to a line of conduct or a task selected by one's spiritual *directeur*.
Blaise communicated his new enthusiasm to Jacqueline, and it also
influenced Etienne Pascal. Curiously enough, at this stage in the
family's history, Jacqueline seems to have been the one most deeply
moved. Although it is important not to minimize the importance of
the changed character and direction of his spiritual life, Blaise did
not—as Gilberte Périer wrote in her biography—give up from this time
forward his scientific interests and work.

As often in his life, he carried on several demanding activities at
once. When Pierre Petit, an amateur scientist and a friend of Etienne
Pascal, paid a visit to the family in 1646, he told them of Torricelli's
experiments with a tube of mercury that had been up-ended in a bowl
that also contained mercury. Etienne and Blaise Pascal and Petit got
the necessary materials together and repeated the experiment successfully. The column of mercury regularly went down part of the length
of the tube and then stopped. What was left in the upper portion
of the tube? Was it air, was it some other matter, or was it, perhaps,
the *vide*? The question and the answer to it had far-reaching implications, since the received view, proposed by the Scholastic philosophers, held that nature as a whole was full and "abhorred" a vacuum.
The experimenters recorded their results without coming to definite
conclusions. After Petit left, Pascal repeated the experiment with many
variations, gathering material that he was to publish later.

Early in the next year (1647) he became engaged for the first time
in a religious polemic. Jacques Forton, sieur de Saint-Ange, newly
arrived in Rouen and seeking a clerical post, caused something of a
stir by his unusual way of treating certain Christian doctrines. He had
very definite ideas about the relation of reason to faith, a subject in
which, as we have seen, the Pascal family had a lively interest. They
stood for a clear separation between the two domains and their objects. But Saint-Ange wanted to reason out Christian dogmas to the
limit, going so far as to attempt a demonstration of the Trinity. Pascal
(then twenty-four years old) and two of his young friends became
involved in the discussion of these matters. They tried to get at least
a partial retraction from Saint-Ange. When he refused, they pursued

the dispute up the ecclesiastical ladder to the archbishop, and Saint-Ange did finally renounce some of his theses.

In the spring of that year, perhaps overburdened as a result of his scientific work, his theological concerns, and his continuing efforts to perfect the *machine arithmétique*, Pascal became seriously ill. He suffered from headaches, stomach pains, and partial paralysis of the legs. Treatment brought some relief, but it was apparently decided that he would try to complete the cure in Paris. Toward the middle of 1647 he returned to the capital, accompanied by Jacqueline.[4]

Research, Controversy, and Reflection (1647–51)

In Paris a new period began in the life of Pascal, and indeed in the life of the family. Both Blaise and Jacqueline showed a new and greater degree of independence. Jacqueline was increasingly intent on becoming a nun at Port-Royal; and Blaise, while taking up some of the old threads of social life in Paris, made important progress in the pursuit of scientific truth and in the deepening of his religious convictions.

On 22 March 1649, two years after the return to Paris, he was granted the *privilège* allowing him exclusive rights to manufacture the arithmetical machine, as he had not yet given up the idea of making and selling it in quantity. He continued energetically his earlier interest in geometry, but of course he was now able to go far beyond the modest "Essai pour les coniques" of 1640. He composed a broadly conceived treatise (or as it turned out in fact, a series of related short *traités*) on conic sections. It was apparently finished in 1648. All of it is lost, with the exception of an introductory section on the generation of conic sections. This remains thanks to the fact that Leibniz, in the process of examining some mathematical papers left by Pascal at his death, decided to make a copy of it for himself.

Pascal's work in physics added greatly to his fame at this time. He published in October of 1647 his *Expériences nouvelles touchant le vide, faites dans des tuyaux, seringues, soufflets et siphons de plusieurs longueurs et figures, avec diverses liqueurs comme vif argent, eau, vin, huile, air, etc., avec un discours sur le même sujet, où est montré qu'un vaisseau si grand qu'on le pourra faire, peut être rendu vide de toutes matières connues en la nature, et qui tombent sous les sens, et quelle force est nécessaire pour faire admettre ce vide.*[5] I cite the entire title, because it evokes so clearly both the kind of experimentation in which Pascal was engaged and also the conclusions to which he came. In the work he presented a carefully argued report of his results. He proved to his satisfaction the existence of the *vide*, rejecting entirely the notion of *matière subtile*—"subtle matter"—proposed by Descartes (with whom Pascal had two inconclusive conversations in September of that year). He retained a modified version of the "horror of the vacuum" theory, for it seemed at that point required if one were to explain the partial suspension of liquids in the apparatus with which he experimented.

The *Expériences nouvelles* led to a controversy with Père Noël, who was rector of the Collège de Clermont and a former teacher of Descartes. In a letter to Pascal he defended vigorously nature's abhorrence of the void in terms and with principles borrowed from Aristotle (more precisely, the Scholastic version of Aristotle then current). His confident conclusion was that a special substance rather like the Cartesian *matière subtile* filled the alleged *vide*. A cycle of refutations began. Pascal composed a lengthy reply, his *Réponse au très bon Révérend Père Noël*. A masterpiece of clarity and logic, it made the inventive imagination and metaphysical agility of his opponent look ridiculous. The letter is not only remarkable for its intellectual qualities as Pascal analyzes the arguments of Noël and marshals his own, but also for traces of that irony to be so brilliantly displayed eight years later in the *Lettres provinciales*. In this, his first polemic encounter with a Jesuit, Pascal was more than a match for his opponent, whose letter offered a good target, with its bits of wisdom concerning the four elements, the four humors, and their respective combinations. Here is Noël's famous definition of light: "la lumière, ou plutôt l'illumination, est un mouvement luminaire des rayons, composés des corps lucides qui remplissent les corps transparents, et ne sont mus luminairement que par d'autres corps lucides."[6] The vicious circle it contains gave Pascal a chance to explain to his eminent adversary how definitions should be framed.

Noël answered in his turn, reasserting that the top of Torricelli's tube contained *matière subtile*, but this time he asked Pascal not to reveal his reply. Since they were both ill, he said, they should wait until they were well and able to discuss the matter orally. Nevertheless, with a certain deviousness, he published under the intriguing title of *Le Plein du vide* a new attack on Pascal's position in which he argued for the "fullness of the void." This led to Pascal's *Lettre* to his friend Le Pailleur, in which he explained his method once more and restated his case. It also provoked a reaction and a letter from Etienne Pascal, who addressed the Jesuit directly in defense of his son.

But Pascal was moving on to the next stage in demolishing the theory according to which nature was, without exception, a *plenum.* Torricelli had assumed that the behavior of the mercury in the tube was due to an equilibrium reached by the volume of mercury and the corresponding column of air. Pascal took up this hypothesis and invented an experiment by which to test it. His basic idea was to measure the height of the column at the foot and at the top of the Puy-de-Dôme near Clermont. After several months of delay the experiment was at last carried out in September of 1648 by his brother-in-law, Florin Périer. He obtained readings of a maximum height in Clermont, a minimum at the top of the mountain, and a series of intermediate readings on the way down, all confirming Pascal's (and Torricelli's) intuition. Périer's report, entitled *Récit de la grande expérience de l'équilibre des liqueurs* [Account of the great experiment on the equilibrium of liquids], and some added commentary by Pascal in a foreword were quickly published. The experiment was then thought to be a model of scientific procedure (and it still is so considered, though it is now clear that Pascal did not take into account all the variables that might affect his results).

One last episode in the affair of the *vide* is worth recalling. In June 1651 Pascal was obliged to defend himself once more against a Jesuit, who accused him indirectly but unmistakably of taking credit for Torricelli's experiment. Pascal's rejoinder came again in the form of a letter, addressed to M. de Ribeyre, a friend of the Pascal family and the person to whom the Jesuit had dedicated his thesis. Pascal explained with some heat what his and Torricelli's respective contributions had been.

The argument and tone of this letter indicate that Pascal sought and enjoyed public recognition of his achievements. Still he could not fail to see that absorption in scientific activity distracted him from other concerns, that it formed an attachment to *le monde.* That was an inclusive term, standing for anything that obscured or interfered with the commandment to love God above everything else and with all one's being. As time passed the tension between the world and his religious beliefs increased. From the time of their return to Paris Pascal and his sister had formed ties with Port-Royal. There Jacqueline came to know well two of the principal nuns, Mère Angélique and Mère Agnès, and she decided that she wished to retire to the convent. She and her brother heard sermons by Singlin, who continued at Port-Royal the tradition of Saint-Cyran.

From a letter of 1648 it is known that Blaise had with Antoine de Rebours, a confessor at the convent, a conversation in which he defended the place of rational arguments in the approach to faith. Perhaps this reflected a desire on his part to justify his continuing involvement with mathematics and physics: reason was not necessarily vain or presumptuous; it could serve other than worldly interests. At any rate the principle at stake was of the utmost importance to Pascal (though it seems not to have been well-received by M. de Rebours), for it reappears in the "Entretien avec M. de Saci" [Conversation with M. de Saci] and it lies at the core of the *Pensées.* Furthermore, it seems to mark an advance over the views expressed in the preface to the *Traité du vide* [Treatise on the vacuum]—dating probably from 1647—where the distinction between the domains of faith and reason is drawn so emphatically. A letter of April 1648 to Gilberte shows Pascal at work on another essential theme in his religious thought, the antithesis between visible and invisible things, the former being related to the latter as images or figures. Thus reason supports faith and things presage the realm of the spirit. We see in these reflections that Pascal was reserving in his mind an important place for a hierarchical way of thinking, in contrast to his approach in science, where reality is conceived as literal and self-contained. Then in November of 1648 he wrote a letter on grace and, specifically, on the efforts it requires in personal life if it is not to be lost: there he was surely pondering a rule that applied to his own life.

For Pascal this was not only a time of scientific success and personal questionings. It coincided with severe strains in the fabric of his family. Having now returned from Rouen to Paris, Etienne Pascal saw how far Jacqueline had gone in the development of a religious vocation, and he began to oppose in no uncertain terms her plan to become a nun. This put him in conflict with Blaise, who sided with his sister. Gilberte, though absent, also supported Jacqueline. The upshot of the discussions, some no doubt tense, was that Jacqueline would not act on her resolution until after the death of her father, whose health had begun to fail.

In the meantime the Fronde, that abortive revolution against the monarchy, was running its course. With armies and brigands in the fields and on the roads, with disorders in Paris, the situation became so bad that the family decided in May of 1649 to go to Clermont temporarily. They stayed for approximately eighteen months, not returning until November of the following year. At Clermont, as at Paris, Jacqueline lived the life of a recluse. She wore black and rarely left her room except to go to church. She made a few translations or paraphrases of Latin hymns, but on the advice of Mère Agnès Arnauld gave up as too worldly this revival of her interest in poetry. Her religious commitment, which had tended from the beginning to be calm and ascetic, stood no doubt in contrast to that of her brother, though exactly what his state of mind was at this time is not clear. His faith was apparently intact, but during the stay in Clermont he wrote nothing, it seems, on religion.

Then came the death of Etienne Pascal, at the age of sixty-three, on 24 September 1651. Gilberte could not be at the bedside because of the birth of a son. Her absence provided the occasion for Pascal to compose a letter to her and her husband on the death of his father. This valuable and moving document is a sermon on the meaning of death for a Christian. Pascal evokes the will of God and need to conform to it. One should accept, even welcome, death as a deliverance from sin and as the consummation of a sacrifice like that of Jesus Christ. The phrasing of the letter mingles words of consolation and of exhortation. One senses deep feeling behind the theological eloquence, but as yet no disposition to renounce the world and its works.

On the Way to the *Mémorial* (1651–54)

The next three years, from the end of 1651 to the end of 1654, were filled with the most varied activities. There were for Pascal some pressing personal concerns having to do with settling his father's estate, facing Jacqueline's entry into Port-Royal, and making financial arrangements that would allow him to live on a suitable footing. Serious difficulties arose in connection with Jacqueline's portion of the estate. Blaise took it over, with a contractual understanding that he would provide her with an income. It was a perfectly legitimate thing to do, but the circumstances changed as she pursued her intention of becoming a nun. Although for a time, before the death of Etienne Pascal, Blaise had been in favor of her project, now he argued against it, and wanted her to stay on with him for a few years. This she refused to do. Both believed that they were right; there were strong feelings on both sides. Early in January she left for the convent without saying good-bye to her brother. Relations between them were still tense in May at the time of her taking of the veil, though he overcame his resentment enough to be present at the ceremony. Difficulties continued over the question of the dowry she was to take to Port-Royal, according to the custom of the order (actually illegal at the time, but followed nonetheless). Finally, on 4 June 1653 the arrangements were completed—still not to the entire satisfaction of Blaise—and the next day Jacqueline made her final vows. As is clear, these discussions and decisions impinged on Pascal's own circumstances, which were not free from strain and uncertainty. He was bringing his resources together, making some investments, and considering plans for the future, which included apparently hopes of an advantageous marriage.

That he was very much engaged in scientific projects during the period from 1652 to 1654 is attested by many signs and results. He busied himself in popularizing his discoveries, refuting his opponents, and in completing and linking his demonstrations. In April of 1652, on the invitation of the duchesse d'Aiguillon, he gave a lecture in her salon on the experiments concerning the *vide* and on the arithmetical machine. In June of the same year he sent one of the machines to Queen Christina of Sweden, and with it a fascinating dedicatory letter. In it he distinguishes clearly and forcefully between the order of worldly realities and power and the order of the mind—a foreshadowing of some decisive passages in the *Pensées*. (He does not, however, refer to the third order, that of the heart, which completes the series.)

These appeals or addresses to an unspecialized public are related to other and more technical work. In 1654 Pascal was finishing his treatise on the equilibrium of liquids (published in 1663) and his treatise on the arithmetical triangle (published in 1665), and it seems likely that a number of shorter "traités" on arithmetic were complete by this time. In the circle frequented by Pascal gambling was a popular diversion. The Chevalier de Méré and Damien Mitton, whom Pascal saw regularly, sought an answer to the question of what to do with money already wagered if a game has to be interrupted. How should it be divided according to what each player might reasonably expect to win (or lose) if the play were continued? Pascal and Fermat saw this as a mathematical problem, and in an exchange of letters from July to October of 1654 worked out a solution that came to be known as *la règle des partis*, or the rule for the division of stakes. Thus were laid the foundations of the calculus of probabilities. In a short "address to the Parisian Academy of Science"—a continuation of the old "Académie Mersenne"—Pascal summed up his scientific activities with a list of works in arithmetic, geometry, and physics that he was composing or had composed, ending with a mention of what he had discovered about the *partis*. It was, he said, a new and astonishing science, the *aleae geometria* or geometry of chance.

The interval from 1651 to 1654 is usually described as the *période mondaine* in Pascal's life. In it he showed a new awareness of society and of the pleasures of social intercourse. Picking up the threads of a relationship going back to his childhood, Pascal became associated with the duc de Roannez, whose position put him in the highest echelon of the nobility. He had been a soldier and had been promoted to the grade of field marshal at the age of twenty-two (he was four years younger than Pascal). Pascal saw him often and is known to have traveled with him and to have stayed occasionally at the Hôtel de Roannez.

In the duke's entourage he came to know the two men just mentioned in connection with the problem of the *partis*: Méré, a self-appointed expert on good manners, and Mitton, a wealthy member of the bourgeoisie with a taste for gambling and a skeptical turn of mind somewhat in the manner of Montaigne. Méré and Mitton presented a challenge to the intelligence and values of Pascal. They were certainly not ignorant; they had principles and taste; they made sense. They were not and felt no need to be mathematicians. Science had no special prestige in their eyes, at least not as part of a gentleman's equipment, nor did either take religion very seriously. By his contacts with these two and with others like them, Pascal seems to have seen the consistency and the appeal of social life as never before. He found himself as a result obliged to make an intellectual adjustment that coincided more or less exactly with a painfully unsettled moral state.

A set of conflicts emerged, with no plain solution in sight. He had originally taken over from his father the idea of a strict separation of reason and faith, experience and authority. There had seemed to be no cause for thinking that the two could not coexist in peace. Contacts with the Jansenists and their kind of religious commitment showed that a conflict was possible. And Pascal had before his eyes the example of his sister, who had been willing to make the radical choice when it became clear to her that faith and vocation were more important than intelligence and talent. It is very likely that Pascal had begun to suspect, as a *géomètre* and as a Christian, that his own situation might lead to a similar outcome. Moreover, he now was encountering vividly another rival to spiritual progress: the attractions and amusements of society—and yet, he knew that they could not be the way he should follow. Late in 1654 he had reached the point where he could conceive of giving up his style of life. The difficulty was that, although he felt an aversion for the world, there was no corresponding pull in the other direction. The alternative had not yet shown itself compellingly, and the initiative for it was out of his hands.

A letter written in September by Jacqueline, whom Pascal was seeing regularly, shows that an inner crisis was brewing. The mounting state of moral detachment and of ennui (in the strong seventeenth-century sense of that word: torment, not boredom) could hardly continue. In the night of 23 November 1654 the process came to a climax. From ten-thirty until about half-past midnight Pascal underwent an ecstatic experience that was decisive for the rest of his life. To remember it he jotted down on a sheet of paper a series of isolated words, phrases, and short sentences. This *mémorial* was found at the time of his death sewed in the lining of his jacket. He had apparently transferred it from garment to garment during the last eight years of his life. Beginning with an evocation of fire and an allusion to the episode of Moses and the burning bush, it moves back and forth from the notation of intimate feelings to biblical references and quotations to fragments of prayer. The two main themes are separation from God that is real and painful and reunion with Him that is real and joyful—though precarious. They are expressed at the highest pitch of insight and emotion. The *mémorial* ends on a note of change and new resolve. "Renonciation totale et douce": so much for the world and the past; "soumission à Jésus-Christ et à mon directeur":[7] so much for the fact and aspiration of a new life.

Discerning, Discovering, and Defending the Truth (1655–59)

The period from the beginning of 1655 to a point early in 1659 (February, to be exact) includes important developments in Pascal's spiritual life, increasing involvement with the views and fate of Port-Royal, and a great broadening of the audience to which he addressed himself in his writings. Pascal spent three weeks in January of 1655 at the convent, joining in the prayers, work, and personal exchanges that characterized the routine of the *solitaires* (the group of remarkable men who had taken up an ascetic life at Port Royal). From this time appears to date the "entretien avec M. de Saci," known to us by the account given in the memoirs of Nicolas Fontaine, Saci's secretary. Pascal is depicted as discussing Montaigne and Epictetus with Saci, the nuns' confessor. The succinct and beautifully turned analyses of the two authors are arranged in the dialectical pattern usually favored by Pascal in his nonmathematical works and utilized to perfection in the *Pensées* and the *Ecrits sur la grâce*. Later in the same year we have a sign of Pascal's growing influence in the sphere of religion on those about him, where he became a sort of spiritual guide to his friend, the duc de Roannez (and, in 1656, to his friend's sister Charlotte, after her conversion). Pascal seemed to have abandoned any ideas he might have had of marriage and to have given up scientific work. But he was still living in *le monde*; he did not assume the regular and austere existence of the *solitaires* of Port-Royal.

In the meantime the tide of controversy between the Jansenists and their opponents, mainly Jesuits, had risen to a new height. By the end of the year 1655 Antoine Arnauld, a member of the Port-Royal group and a *docteur* of the Sorbonne, was being strongly attacked for his defense of Jansenius. The debates centered on the notion of grace and on five propositions, supposedly extracted from Jansenius's treatise on Saint Augustine. (The propositions were condemned by Rome in 1653.) Arnauld had written and published two letters on grace and communion, and early in 1656 he had prepared still another. His friends thought it likely to be ineffective, however, because he wrote in a technical style not very appealing to a general audience. Pascal chanced to be at Port-Royal at the time, and he was asked to try his hand. The result was the first of the *Lettres provinciales*, which purported to be written by an observer in Paris who wished to explain to a friend in the provinces what the controversy at the Sorbonne was about. An immediate and a very great success, this letter was followed by others, at the rate of one or two per month, until March of 1657. By then eighteen letters had appeared. In them Pascal ranged over a whole spectrum of problems—moral, logical, and theological—with nearly unflagging energy and brilliance. He first portrayed (letters 1–4) the Jesuits and their sympathizers, evoking them with a fine sense of the comic element in their ineptness and contradictions; then in the middle letters (5–16) he concentrated on the laxity he saw in their books of casuistry and on the unworthiness of their intrigues; and in the last letters (17–18), which are directly addressed to Père Annat, a noted Jesuit and Louis XIV's confessor, Pascal attacked the *compagnie* for their violently partisan spirit and slanderous tactics. They had invented, he thought, the issue of heresy in the theology of Jansenius and used it to further the ends and influence of their order.

The letters appeared anonymously: only a few people knew the secret of their authorship. In fact, there was an air of mystery and revolt surrounding the whole project, and various attempts were made to interfere with it. Arnauld and Nicole supplied Pascal with principles, arguments, and crucial texts. It should, therefore, be kept in mind that the letters were in an important sense a work of collaboration. Taken together they form an unsurpassed model of polemical style and of popularization. Historians of the French language agree in saluting them as a monument in the evolution of French prose.

In 1657 a new condemnation of Jansenius came from Rome, and the French *Assemblée du clergé* [Assembly of the clergy] proposed that all members of the clergy sign an affidavit to the effect that they adhered to this judgment and repudiated the five propositions. Père Pirot, on the Jesuit side, published an *Apologie pour les casuistes* [Defense of the casuists] in December of the same year. These events revived and refueled the quarrel. Again Pascal took part, along with Arnauld and Nicole; he is probably the author of the *Factum pour les curés de Paris* [Pamphlet in behalf of the priests of Paris] and of three other texts directed in particular against the work of Pirot. The controversy it had caused was officially ended in 1659, when Pope Alexander VII put the *Apologie pour les casuistes* on the *Index*. The question of the affidavit or *formulaire*, however, continued to be a bone of contention.

Pascal's activities in support of Port-Royal and its version of Augustinianism did not cause him to lose interest completely in mathematical problems, nor did he, in his partial withdrawal from society, cut all his ties with his scientific friends. At the request of Arnauld he undertook to prepare in 1657 or 1658 an *Eléments de géométrie* for the Port-Royal schools. Although the result was not judged to be satisfactory and the project was set aside, two texts that appear to be preliminary versions of the preface are extant. Since they were first published in the eighteenth century they have had the general title, *De l'esprit géométrique* [On the geometrical mind]. In them Pascal treated the arts of demonstration and persuasion, which he apparently conceived as capable of assimilation into a single technique. Moreover, he kept in touch with Roberval, Carcavi, and other friends of a scientific or mathematical turn of mind. In the year 1658—as the story goes, and it is attested by members of Pascal's family and others—he was suffering one day from a very painful toothache and to distract himself he turned to the problem of the "roulette." In concrete terms this is the curve that is produced by a nail in the circumference of a wheel as it moves over a flat roadbed. (It was known more technically as the "cycloïde.") His intense concentration was doubly fruitful: he found the formulas for the properties of the curve, and the toothache disappeared.

Pascal might not have published his findings, but he was encouraged to do so by the duc de Roannez, who happened to know that a project for an apology of the Christian religion was germinating at that time in his friend's mind. He proposed an international contest, with a reward to the winner, to see if anyone else could solve the problems of the *roulette*. The idea was that this would show Pascal as someone who could argue the cause of faith and who knew also—and perfectly—the powers and limits of reason. In execution the project went wrong in several ways. After launching the contest, Pascal discovered that his friend Roberval had already solved the first four of the six problems posed. Then there were protests from contestants, who criticized the conditions for submitting solutions as unfair, and even ventured to accuse Pascal of using the papers received in reaching his own formulations. For his part Pascal aroused bad feeling by his merciless treatment of errors he located in the responses of contestants and by the patronizing tone of infallibility that he took in the whole affair. No prizes were awarded, and one can doubt that much was accomplished for religion by this episode, though the cause of geometry and of infinitesimal calculus undoubtedly benefited from it.

Between the publication of the fifth and sixth *Provinciales* an extraordinary thing happened at Port-Royal. It had many consequences for Pascal and his thought. His ten-year-old niece, Marguerite

Périer, was a pupil at the convent. For two years she had suffered from an abcess located between one of her eyes and her nose. No one had been able to cure it, and the doctors talked of trying to cauterize it. Then on 24 March 1656 a reliquary said to contain a piece of the Crown of Thorns was brought to the convent for veneration. At the close of the ceremony one of the sisters picked up the reliquary and touched Marguerite's eye with it. That night the abcess appeared to be cured, and a week later the cure was confirmed as a fact by a doctor, who declared it to be a miracle. There followed examinations by doctors and investigations by church authorities. By the end of October what had happened was ratified as being, indeed, miraculous. Pascal's emotion was understandably great: he felt that God had shown a sign of favor toward his family.

The miracle strengthened his resolve to continue the series of letters against the Jesuits, but it also stirred him to study and to think about the whole subject of miracles. From meditations on the "miracle de la Sainte Epine" he went on to examine instances of miracles in the Bible. He saw the value of attested miracles in apologetic reasoning, and at one time he seems to have thought of writing a letter on miracles. Then the plan grew to include questions of flawed human nature and the ways by which it might be redeemed. The upshot was that in 1657 and 1658 Pascal wrote down most of what we know as his *Pensées*, intending these fragments as preparatory material for a full-scale apology of the Christian religion.

He began the task of classifying the bits and pieces and putting some order into his argument, and this shaping process, obviously inspired by a coherent plan, led to a series of twenty-eight groups of papers, each of which had its own subject heading or title. Taken as a whole, they present a position that is reasonably sequential. These fragments—about four hundred from a total corpus of approximately eight hundred fragments—form the heart of the apology. (I am adopting here the enumeration proposed in 1976 by Philippe Sellier.) But it seems clear that the work of classifying fragments and of rounding out the presentation continued intermittently into 1660, and even beyond, in spite of Pascal's poor health. For the period from 1659 until his death in 1662 was nothing like the preceding two years of great activity. Much of the time was spent in what his sister Gilberte described as a "langueur pitoyable," a state that made sustained intellectual work impossible. He once said that it would take ten years of good health to bring his project to fulfillment.[8]

Toward Perfect Charity (1659–62)

From this period of serious illness comes Pascal's "Prière pour demander à Dieu le bon usage des maladies." He had often said to Gilberte that illness is the natural state of Christians. This prayer expresses in passionate but lucid periods a great effort to find a Christian meaning in his own suffering, to discern the divine will, and to submit to it wholly and trustfully. Pascal asks God to dispose of his health and his sickness, his life and his death, first for the glory of God, then for his salvation and for the good of the church and the saints.

This attitude forms part of an intense spiritual regime into which he now entered. He studied the Bible until he all but knew it by heart; he participated fervently in devotions; above all he sought to rid himself of pride and of all worldly feelings. As he humbled himself, he turned to the poor, helping them with money, visiting them, taking them into his house. He did not, however, cut himself off completely from friends. There is evidence of continuing relations with the Roannez and with Domat, with Mme de Sablé, with Arnauld and Nicole. He took the time to compose three short "Discours sur la condition des Grands" specifically for the duc de Chevreuse, a pupil of Lancelot at Port-Royal, though they set forth the illusions and temptations to which all those of noble birth are subject, and to lay down the principles needed for seeing such rank in its true light as a contingent privilege. But the letter of 10 August 1660 to Fermat shows decisively that purely intellectual interests had been put aside. Pascal writes that geometry is a valuable way of learning to reason correctly, that it is, indeed, the highest exercise of the mind; but for all that it is only a *métier*, and ultimately useless. This summary judgment is surrounded by polite formulas addressed to Fermat himself. Pascal's convictions and his strict rule of charity in relations with others did not exclude *honnêteté*, that exquisite civility so prized in seventeenth-century French society.

The issue of the formulary or affidavit condemning Jansenius erupted again in 1661. In February of that year the Assembly of the Clergy decided that every *ecclésiastique* and every teacher must sign the document. A serious difference of opinion arose between Pascal and his close friends Arnauld and Nicole. They saw a way of recognizing and accepting *de jure* the verdict of the bishops and the pope: they might condemn the heretical doctrine imputed to Jansenius, but would not feel bound to think or assert that the doctrine was expressed in fact, *de facto*, in Jansenius's *Augustinus*. Pascal showed himself in this instance to be more Jansenist than the Jansenists, for he believed that the dispute had reached a point where it was no longer possible to maintain the distinction between principle and fact. To him (as apparently to his sister Jacqueline) signing the formulary meant sacrificing not only Jansenius but also Saint Augustine, Saint Paul, and the true Catholic doctrine of grace. Being a layman, he was / under no obligation to sign it. However, the radical disagreement with his friends led him to withdraw from all further theological controversy and to give himself entirely to works of charity.

In the last months of his life we catch another glimpse of the practical turn of mind that we associate with his experiments and with the invention of the *machine arithmétique*. He joined an undertaking with Roannez and three others to provide, by means of carriages charging a low fare, a public transportation service in Paris. The scheme was put into effect in March of 1662 and proved to be successful. Pascal's intention was to use his share of the proceeds for his work with the poor.

Unfortunately his health deteriorated further. His situation was a difficult one: living with him was a family of *pauvres* that he had taken in. Gilberte visited him regularly to see to his needs. But he had to be moved at last (on 29 June) to her house. He suffered from severe intestinal pains and headaches. Although the doctors were optimistic about the effects of their medicines, bloodlettings, and purgations, Pascal had little confidence in them; he felt that his end was near. In the night of 17 August he received communion, after which he said, "Que Dieu ne m'abandonne jamais!" ("May God never abandon me!") Those were his last words. He died at one in the morning of 19 August 1662 at the age of thirty-nine.

Chapter Two

The Mathematical and Physical Works

The Mathematical Treatises: Introduction

Most students and readers, when they take up Pascal, usually concentrate their attention on the *Lettres provinciales*, the *Pensées*, and a few shorter *opuscules* directly related to those two larger works. They often neglect the mathematical and physical works, though they may honor them with a passing comment and a casual eulogy. In this there is a certain danger. When one is dealing with a thinker like Pascal, who is very conscious of method and logical consistency, one expects to find a noticeable degree of unity in all aspects of his work. Even if this unity should not reach into details but turn out to be that of a more or less well-stated opposition, it would be worth noting, for opposed views and terms imply and define each other. And so I have decided to include here a treatment of these scientific works, in the belief that they help us to understand the others and to place them in their proper light.

Let us first survey the mathematical writings. They have a certain priority over the investigations in physics, since the latter depend from the point of view of method on the prior existence of mathematical tools that may be applied in an experimental situation. Among Pascal's complete works one finds about three dozen items that fit into the general category of mathematical treatises. It is not easy to establish a precise chronology for them, or to classify their contents in a truly satisfactory way. In a dedicatory letter written in 1654 to the circle of Parisian mathematicians and scientists whom he knew and admired, Pascal summarizes what he had done to that date. He had worked in geometry on conic sections and in arithmetic on numbers and number series; and he had solved the problem of the *règle des partis*—which is essentially a technique of arithmetical calculation. The so-called *triangle arithmétique* [arithmetical triangle], a way of tabulating and relating number series, fascinated him later that year. After the conversion of November 1654, there comes a gap in his mathematical researches. But on one occasion (we mentioned it above) early in 1658 he was suffering from a toothache that made it impossible for him to sleep. As Gilberte puts it, "Mais quel moyen a un esprit comme le sien d'être éveillé et de ne penser à rien."[1] He fell to thinking about some unsolved problems having to do with the *roulette* or cycloid curve. One idea followed another and he suddenly realized that he had arrived at the solutions. These discoveries led to sixteen varied yet often repetitive items in the catalog of mathematical works (and also to the contest mentioned in chapter 1), plus seven related items on the subject of curved lines and their properties.

Looking at his productions in the order of time, we can thus say that Pascal carried on research in geometry and arithmetic over a period of fourteen years from 1640 to 1654, culminating in a spurt of rapid work on the arithmetical triangle, and that—four years later— he took up again as a kind of interlude a new set of problems in geometry.

It is customary to speak of Pascal's "mathematical treatises" as if they formed a homogeneous group of works and as if their characteristics were obvious. This usual phrase is doubly troublesome. First, Pascal's first "treatise," for example, the "Essai pour les coniques," is much more the statement of an intended program of investigation than a report of results; and the other documents come in various shapes and sizes. He may put his thoughts in a "lettre," a set of "réflexions," a "note," a "récit," or an "histoire" (as in the involved account of the contest dealing with the cycloid curve). Second, the word "treatise" is likely to call up in our minds the idea of a technical, long, and systematic work that treats a broad problem area. Technical these treatises certainly are—and aspire to be. However, they are not long, in most cases amounting only to a half-dozen pages or less (of course the way the texts are set up in a particular edition affects such a count). Nor are they systematic in the broad sense of that term. The exception was, it would seem, the lost treatise on conic sections, the manuscript of which Leibniz saw and studied. (We are indebted to him, as I mentioned in the preceding chapter, that we have a copy of the beginning of this treatise, the pages that explain and list the types of conic sections.) The rest of the lot have more the character of investigations *ad hoc* addressed to particular topics. They initiate lines of inquiry rather than develop them exhaustively.

In fact, it is interesting to note how often one runs onto passages like the following. These are the last two sentences of the treatise on the divisibility of numbers:

> Il serait facile de justifier ces deux règles et d'en obtenir d'autres. Mais si j'ai touché à ce sujet c'est parce que je cédais à l'attrait de la nouveauté; maintenant je m'arrête de peur de fatiguer le lecteur en entrant dans trop de détails. (89)[2]

Or he may allude to findings in hand but omitted because of their very quantity:

> C'est par ce problème que j'avais décidé d'achever mon traité, non sans regret, je dois le dire, car j'ai en ma possession bien des résultats encore; mais, devant une telle abondance, je me suis bien forcé de me limiter.... (83)[3]

Or, again, as at the end of the general treatise on the *roulette*, he feels content if he has shown the way to be followed, if he has formulated the method for the solution of difficulties: "Il sera sur cela facile à tout le monde de trouver les calculs de tous ces cas, par le moyen de ces méthodes" (171).[4]

Mathematics and Reality

A systematic picture of arithmetic and geometry does not emerge from these documents. The demonstrations presented in them do, however, overlap and interlock. A cumulative effect is distinctly noticeable in several places, and Pascal uses the results and methods found in one or more prior treatises to validate what he does at a later point in his inquiries. This is very evident in the papers relative to the *roulette*, where explicit and important cross-references abound. The interdependence of these texts, coupled with Pascal's constant drive for generality in conclusions and for wide applicability in methods, gives us further reason to suspect that by taking account of the scientific as well as the theological and apologetic writings we may uncover unifying ideas and devices otherwise difficult to see. Here we cannot go into details, but we can study the logical derivation of the problems attacked and the lines of thought to which they give rise.

Certain things must be made clear from the start. In the first place, mathematics was not for Pascal what it is for many today: ultimately a matter of conventions that fix what one will study and how one will study it. He probably would not have accepted the conversion of mathematics into symbolic logic, into a science of symbols, as some have recently done. And it is quite unlikely that he could ever have agreed with a statement like the famous one made by Bertrand Russell, to the effect that mathematicians do not know what they are talking about or whether what they are saying about it is true.

On the contrary, mathematics has a real subject matter that is given in nature: quantity. Of course quantity is found in things, and things may be understood by reference to it, but quantity is in itself subject to investigation apart from physics. It has a *nature* and it has the *properties* that derive therefrom; it is a locus of certain fixities. These steady aspects of quantity are what make it susceptible of scientific study and what make it possible to determine whether what we say about quantity is true or false.

Discontinuous Quantity: Numbers

True knowledge in mathematics falls into two inquiries, geometry and arithmetic, because the subject matter itself is either continuous (as in lines, planes, or spheres) or discontinuous (as in numbers). Let us discuss numbers first and then the figures of geometry. This order will bring us easily to some important questions of intellectual method that have implications for Pascal's thought as a whole.

First, a point about the notation of numbers. Pascal is aware of the conventional bases of his (and our) numbering system. He mentions at least one other possible base, using twelve instead of ten as the means of setting the cyclical element in counting. But the reference is made in passing, and all his arithmetical treatises are expressed in terms of the decimal system.

What is there about numbers that interests him? By means of what concepts are they grasped and investigated? As we might have expected from the basic intuitions about quantity to which I have just referred, he focuses his attention on their natures and properties. In my opinion it is not possible to understand his treatises without observing that distinction. Not that we should try to fix the meaning of the two terms in some metaphysical way: that is something that Pascal does not himself bother to do. "Nature" corresponds to what the number is, to its definition; and the "properties" are traits regularly correlated with the distinct natures and may be thought of as deriving from them. Thus numbers are odd or even, they have factors and roots, they are divisible, and so on. Pascal's aim is to discover formulas for identifying these properties and for stating any regularities discernible in them.

The "Remarque préliminaire" of *De Numeris multiplicibus*—a treatise on the divisibility of numbers—starts out with a mathematical commonplace and an easy example:

> Rien de plus connu en arithmétique que la proposition d'après laquelle un multiple quelconque de 9 se compose de chiffres dont la somme est elle-même un multiple de 9. Si, par exemple, on additionne les chiffres dont se compose 18, double de 9, on trouve $1 + 8 = 9$. (84)[5]

Pascal is beginning here the analysis of a property, divisibility by 9, that may be affirmed of some numbers. He draws our attention to an easy and received way of determining the case for any particular number: we change our viewpoint, and consider the number as the *sum of its digits* rather than as a *multiple of 9*; and if that sum is divisible by 9, so is the original number. Then he offers us a less obvious example: "Ainsi, 1719 est un multiple de 9, parce que la somme $1 + 7 + 1 + 9$ ou 18 de tous ses chiffres est elle-même divisible par 9.[6] With the situation defined, and the commonplace level of understanding summed up, Pascal is ready to indicate the direction his own thought will take: "Bien que cette règle soit communément employée, je ne crois pas que personne jusqu'à présent en ait donné une démonstration ni ait cherché à en généraliser le principe" (84).[7] That sets the program for this treatise: to demonstrate and to generalize. He promises to justify the rule of 9, to show how other and similar cases may be treated (already a start of generalization) and then to push the process further: "j'exposerai aussi une méthode générale qui permet de reconnaître, à la simple inspection de la somme de ses chiffres, si un nombre est divisible par un autre nombre quelconque . . ." (84).[8] And one might have supposed that the process would end there. But Pascal's acute sense of possibilities, of the exhaustive list of possibilities, is always vigilant:

cette méthode ne s'applique pas seulement à notre système décimal de numération (système qui repose sur une convention, d'ailleurs assez malheureuse, et non sur une nécessité naturelle, comme le pense le vulgaire), mais elle s'applique encore sans défaut à tout système de numération ayant pour base tel nombre qu'on voudra.... (84)[9]

A great deal of Pascal is contained in this brief passage. His thought shows so often this same inner movement: from what the *vulgaire* thinks to what the *savant* knows; from a supposed "nature" to a convention, from the convention to an underlying and authentic nature that is reducible to a formula; from the particular to the general; from the fundamental but unelaborated theme to the treatise, where everything latent is brought into the open and developed according to a strict order.

Another important property of numbers is their capacity to form series. The generative principle of the series may vary. One of Pascal's favorite ways of exploiting numbers thus arranged is to use repeated additions. Actually simple repetition forms a series: (a) 1, 1, 1, 1, 1, etc. But if one adds something to form the successive members of the chain, one gets series like the following: (b) 1, 2, 3, 4, 5 (where one or a unit is added to each preceding member to arrive at the following member: $2 = 1 + 1$; $3 = 2 + 1$, etc.); or (c) 1, 3, 6, 10, 15 (where, instead of adding one to each preceding term, we add each member of the "natural" series—1, 2, 3, 4, 5—to the member that precedes it: $3 = 1 + 2$; $6 = 3 + 3$; $10 = 6 + 4$; $15 = 10 + 5$, etc.). If we take 1, 3, 6, 10, 16, etc. and treat it as before (in c), we have: (d) 1, 4, 10, 20, 35, etc.

It is essential to note that there is no end to the number of series one can form by using this additive principle: next comes (e) 1, 5, 15, 35, 70, etc.; and then (f) 1, 6, 21, 56, 126, etc.; and (g) 1, 7, 28, 84, 210, etc.; and (h) 1, 8, 36, 120, 330, etc. "Et ainsi à l'infini," writes Pascal. In other words this play with number series brings us very quickly face to face with one of the key notions not just here but elsewhere. In the fragment on the wager in the *Pensées*, that we can know the existence of the *infini en nombre* without knowing its nature (is it odd or even?—there is no way to decide) prefigures our situation in faith, where we know that an infinite being exists, but there is no way for us to grasp his unlimited nature. In fact, there are two infinites at work in the present context: the one Pascal refers to explicitly and the one that is masked by the "etc."

at the end of each sample series. For each one can run on endlessly, continually applying the formula of the series to generate a new member. One might, perhaps, speak of a *vertical* infinite, as the list grows unceasingly longer, and of a *horizontal* infinite, as the sequence of terms grows unceasingly in the number of terms included.

Each of these progressions forms, I have said, a series, but Pascal uses consistently the term "ordre," referring to "nombres du premier ordre" (series *a* above); "nombres du second ordre" (series *b* above); "nombres du troisième ordre" (series *c* above), and so on down the line. Thus another distinctive and basic notion, that of *ordre*, comes into view: it, too, is indispensable to Pascal. Without it, as I shall show later, his panoramic view of the universe and its contents—bodies, minds, hearts, and their correlatives—would collapse in confusion.

We saw above, with the problem of divisibility in numbers, that one line of thought favored by Pascal leads him from a single case to several or many cases to all cases, that is, along a line of *increasing generality*. There is another and equally characteristic direction his reasoning may take: a movement from simple elements to composites of *greater and greater scope*. The "triangle arithmétique"—Pascal did not invent this figure, but he was obviously fascinated by it—illustrates perfectly this second procedure, and enables us to note another aspect of his work in arithmetic.

Just as factors when added or multiplied produce numbers whose properties may then be studied systematically, so numbers, as we have just seen, may in turn produce progressions or series. The next step in this cumulative trend gathers the numerical "orders" into a unified ensemble. This becomes possible if one starts with two lines forming a right angle, divides it into equal lengths, and connects the resulting points so as to make a triangle composed of boxes or "cellules." Then the numerical series may be inscribed, number by number, in the square spaces. Each order is placed under the preceding order in such a way that the first terms (1 in each case) are in a line reading from top to bottom at the left of the figure, as shown below:

Arithmetical Triangle

	1	2	3	4	5	6	7	8	9	10
1	1	1	1	1	1	1	1	1	1	1
2	1	2	3	4	5	6	7	8	9	
3	1	3	6	10	15	21	28	36		
4	1	4	10	20	35	56	84			
5	1	5	15	35	70	126				
6	1	6	21	56	126					
7	1	7	28	84						
8	1	8	36							
9	1	9								
10										

This done, we have a new object of study, the group or ensemble of numerical orders. Numbers are now seen with reference to other numbers in a context of systematic and repeating relationships. This is so because of the fact that the rules of addition according to which Pascal constituted the series were systematic and repetitive, and because he inscribes the series in the triangle so as to line them up in a particular way. For example, as soon as we move into the triangle (away from the borders above and on the left), every number turns out to be the sum of the number in the cell immediately to the left of it *plus* the number in the square immediately above it.

In short, this ensemble has a "nature" and consequent "properties" (in the rough sense I have suggested), and Pascal can now exercise his ingenuity in demonstrating and generalizing propositions about the rows and ranks of cells and their contents. He states and proves nineteen "conséquences." The first eleven concern *equalities* and the remaining eight have as their subject several *proportions*, and of course they will be found in every arithmetical triangle.

At this point we may note another emergence of the infinite. The triangle with which Pascal is working has the number 1 as the generating element in the first cell. However, as he points out, this is arbitrary; and any other number could occupy the space and generate another set of orders. And so this particular triangle is merely one of an *infinite number* of similar figures, each stretching endlessly in two directions, horizontally along each row and vertically down the list of orders.

But, to return to the triangle at hand: it is not simply an object of theoretical curiosity. Much more, Pascal thinks, can be done, if one goes on working along the line laid down: "On peut tirer de là beaucoup d'autres proportions que je supprime, parce que chacun les peut facilement conclure, et que ceux qui voudront s'y attacher en trouveront peut-être de plus belles que celles que je pourrais donner" (54).[10] Such a concluding note is almost a refrain at the end of the mathematical treatises: he has only begun to develop the implications of this triangular arrangement of numbers. A new treatise follows that buckles precisely onto the preceding one. He calls it *Divers usages du triangle arithmétique*: "Après avoir donné les proportions qui se rencontrent entre les cellules et les rangs des Triangles arithmétiques, je passe à divers usages de ceux dont le générateur est l'unité" (54).[11] Even here he cannot resist adding at the very start an endorsement of the triangle and its "usages:" "Mais j'en laisse bien plus que je n'en donne: c'est une chose étrange combien il est fertile en propriétés."[12]

The first use of the triangle we have already noticed: it serves to gather into a single, open-ended scheme all numbers and the strands to which they give rise. But Pascal wants to use it for formulating and solving specific problems. The second subdivision of the *traité* shows how it can deal with *combinaisons*, that is, situations where a group of factors are given (A, B, C, D, for example) and the aim is to determine how many selections of two or more different factors can be made from the group. Before writing this treatise, Pascal had determined the *règle des partis* (it was developed in the letters exchanged with Fermat in the summer of 1654). Now he sees the possibility of utilizing the triangle for making these calculations. Finally, in the fourth section of the treatise he expounds a way of finding on the triangle answers to problems having to do with raising binomial expressions (like a $+$ 1, a $-$ 1) to various powers.

It is not difficult to see in general how and why the *triangle arith-*

métique works. It is something like a *machine arithmétique* without moving parts. It includes potentially every number out to infinity. The numbers have been formed into regular progressions. As such they are inserted into a regular geometrical figure made up of rows and ranks of cells, any one of which may be located by reference to divisions in the original lines that bound the two closed sides of the figure. Since every number appears—or will appear—at some location in the triangle, it must be true that the numerical data of any problem involving arithmetic calculations are on the triangle (in what we might call the input square or squares), and equally true that the numerical solution is on it as well. Now there is nothing magical about the triangle; some thought on the part of the user is presupposed. One must approach it as Pascal does. He already has solutions, for example, to the problem of the *combinaisons* and of the *partis*. The task is to identify the relevant input square(s) and the relevant output square(s), and then to state the relationships of those squares in terms of their relative positions. That statement, in view of the fact that the same relationship is repeated over and over again on the triangle, becomes a formula for deriving answers by inspection. In short, the triangle makes it possible to translate strictly arithmetical terms and statements into terms and statements that define relative positions on a diagram.

Continuous Quantity: Figures

Pascal's work in geometry falls into two main divisions, or more precisely, concerns two main subject matters: (1) that pertaining to conic sections and (2) that pertaining to the *roulette* or cycloid curve and the various figures—plane and solid—associated with it. Actually very little remains of the first set of treatises. There is the youthful "Essai pour les coniques" of 1640, but it is hardly more than a beginning and a sketch of work to be done. In the so-called "Adresse" of 1654 Pascal refers to a complete treatise on conic sections, described as entirely finished and ready for publication. Here, again, details are lacking. Probably this is an allusion to the manuscripts reviewed by Leibniz at the request of Etienne Périer, Pascal's nephew, who sought advice as to whether the papers were in a state fit for publication. From the letter written by Leibniz on 30 August 1676 we learn that the documents contained six treatises in all on the subject; and through his interest and efforts we have not only a short résumé of the contents of them all, but also the text of the first, on the "Generatio conisectionum" [Generation of conic sections], which Leibniz copied for his own use.[13] All of the originals are lost.

This short piece, consisting of thirty paragraphs (six definitions, plus twenty-four corollaries and scholia) is fascinating for several reasons. For one thing, it gives a concise and finished example of the *esprit de géométrie* at work, showing beautifully how a mathematical edifice—as Pascal conceives it—must be grounded on a few principles made perfectly explicit at the outset. In this his procedure is the antithesis of what one expects from what he calls in the *Pensées* the *esprit de finesse* [intuitive mind], which starts characteristically from a large number of principles in a situation that is already complex. Of course, for these conic sections to be generated, there must first be a cone. With (1) a circle, (2) a fixed point in space (not in the plane of the circle), and (3) a straight line through the fixed point and through the circumference of the circle, Pascal is ready to begin. He imagines the line as proceeding around the circumference of the circle; and by this movement it generates the conic surface. The cone itself he defines as the space contained on the inside of the surface. Note that the surface and the volume stretch to infinity: they are not terminated by the plane of the circle.

To be precise, we have two cones extending upward and downward from the single point that serves as the summit. (It would be just as true to say that one extends to the left and the other to the right; the important thing is the antithetical relationship of the two parts that make up what is in fact a single figure.) In a way the figure or image resembles the one underlying the famous passage on the two infinites in the *Pensées*, except that there one is small and the other large, while here both termini are infinitely large; and the consideration of man and his physical and moral status at the midpoint of the contrasted magnitudes is completely absent. Still, these two infinites that start at the same point and balance each other perfectly bring into the geometrical discussion a Pascalian touch of dialectic and paradox.

Pascal's intellectual imagination continues, introducing next a plane that—like the conic surface—is of infinite extent. The two figures will meet. "Par conséquent un plan infini en position quelconque rencontre nécessairement une surface conique en position quelconque" (39; translated from the Latin).[14] The plane will necessarily cut the cone, and it may do so in six different ways, producing six distinct types of sections: a point, a straight line, an angle, an *antobole* (or closed figure), a parabola, or a hyperbola. Exactly at this moment the *generatio conisectionum* is complete, for the subject matter of the treatise has come into view. The rest of the inquiry will study the natures and develop the properties of these six geometrical entities.

One further observation suggests itself. Pascal is always in control—like some demiurge—of this process whereby infinite surfaces and spaces are delimited and divided. The result is a series of artifacts. Likewise, as we shall see later in more detail, he controls the conditions of the inquiry, since it is he who decides that axiomatic analysis and deductive statement are what he will engage in. In thinking over the bulk of Pascal's work, one cannot help being struck by the varying relations he has to *what* he takes up for study and *how* he studies it. The beings of geometry are made, whereas those of nature are given; and both of these subject matters, when adequately approached, require a method based on sense (or imagination) and reason. But when nature and man are seen as creation and creature, they and their Creator are given, not made (by man, that is); and however much one may have recourse to the experience of sense and reason, the only adequate method is one that bases itself on authority and Scripture.

Let us now examine in somewhat more detail how Pascal goes about investigating his geometrical subject matter. We can make no claim here of following out a psychological process, but we can see how certain inevitable factors are chosen and specified. He necessarily has some idea of what he is looking for. It is useful to cite at this point a few lines from the "Essai pour les coniques."

> En suite de ces trois lemmes et de quelques conséquences d'iceux, nous donnerons des éléments coniques complets, à savoir toutes les propriétés des diamètres et côtés droits, des tangentes, etc., la restitution presque du cône sur toutes les données, la description des sections de cône par points, etc. (36)[15]

The résumé drawn up by Leibniz after examining Pascal's manuscripts has a similar list of topics. Commenting on the third *traité*, he says that it contains an explanation of the properties of the centers and diameters of conic sections. In the fourth treatise he finds a sequel to the third; "quelques belles propriétés universellement conçues, touchant les proportions des droites menées à la section conique; et c'est de là que dépend tout ce qu'on peut dire des ordonnées."[16] The fifth treatise contains further treatment of points and lines in their contacts with conic sections.

To get these results Pascal approaches the sections via a related six-sided figure. According to Leibniz, the first treatise develops the remarkable properties of something Pascal calls the "hexagramme mystique." It seems that every such *hexagramme* corresponds to a conic section, and vice versa. The applications of this six-sided figure appear, says Leibniz, in the following treatises. Thus, in a heuristic step prior to everything else Pascal invents or discovers an instrument, a sort of handle, by which to take hold of his subject matter in a fruitful way. Here, by solving the relationship between conic sections and a set of quite different figures (hexagrams), he locates a path that leads to many further solutions. One is reminded of the *triangle arithmétique* in his discussion of numbers and number series, or, in a much more distant context, of the recourse to original sin as the great explanatory principle when one deals with the many paradoxes of human conduct.

This hexagram functions at various decisive points according to the requirements of a method based on two assumptions: (1) that words and things are distinct; words may belie things, and so the problem of finding the truth reduces essentially to the problem of finding a way to bring words into correspondence with things; and (2) that achieving such a result calls for the use of a technique capable of matching sequences in words with sequences in things. Here is what I mean. In its verbal, discursive aspect Pascal's method requires him to generate definitions, demonstrations, and conclusions, arranged in linear order, with occasional corollaries or remarks added in parallel, so to speak. Apart from such a verbal arrangement truth cannot be stated. But neither can it be stated apart from the natural sequence of parts in the subject matter itself. In other words, in its referential aspect the method takes up the relevant figures step by step, moving (1) from the generation of the conic sections (2) to the general mode of attack on them as problems (3) to the properties of their centers and diameters (4) to the properties of tangents and secants associated with them. Then in the sixth—and transitional—treatise Pascal treats the subject of the *lieu solide* ("le fruit de la doctrine des sections coniques," says Leibniz),[17] where the subject matter opens onto the solution of problems in solid geometry. The points, lines, and two-dimensional surfaces here investigated become presuppositions and stand in an elaborate proportional relationship to another order of geometrical reality—solids. Thus is the essential aim of the method realized—by translating sequences known in the subject matter into antecedents and consequents expressed in discourse; and thus the indeterminacy of language (it may tell the truth about things or not) is overcome.

Measuring the Roulette

The problems connected with the so-called *roulette* or cycloid curve gave rise to an unwieldy collection of documents. It comprises a circular letter announcing the contest; letters exchanged between Pascal and contestants (specifically, Père Lalouère and Sir Christopher Wren), and between Pascal and Carcavi, who headed the committee of judges in the contest; a history of the *roulette* as a subject of study; a sequel to the history; an account of the examination of the contest results; a number of short treatises more or less clearly related to the *roulette*; still other treatises dealing with the measurement of certain other curves. I intend here to treat this sprawling mass of materials under the headings used before: subject matter, principles, and method; and I shall be mainly concerned with the *roulette* and with notions that have echoes or parallels elsewhere in Pascal's work.

Galileo, Roberval, Descartes, Fermat, and Torricelli had aready studied the curve in question. It is the path followed by a point on the circumference of a turning wheel, or as Pascal says even more concretely, "le chemin que fait en l'air le clou d'une roue quand elle roule de son mouvement ordinaire."[18] The situation is actually a little more complicated than that. The curved line is considered as serving, along with its axis and base (which are determined with reference to the diameter of the wheel and the ground on which it is traveling), to enclose a surface; and this surface, when rotated on its axis 'or its base, produces a solid figure. These are the principal subjects under study, but in the course of the discussion derived or related figures appear, such as arcs of circles, squares, triangles, cylindrical triangles and squares (that is, inscribed on a cylindrical surface).

Once the figure to be investigated is before him, Pascal looks for principles by means of which its properties may be discovered. In the documents relating to the contest questions and in the treatises in which he explains in various ways what he did, we can recover his procedure and see what he found fruitful points of departure to be.

His aim was to find what he calls the *dimension* or measurement-formula for the surface, and also the formula for its center of gravity and, then, to find the same two things for the two "demi-solides" produced by the half turns of the original surface on the axis and on the base. To arrive at the solutions, he must engage in various summations of parts that go to make up the whole figures with which he is working. The question then becomes, *what* elements precisely will enter into these additions, and beyond that question still another looms: how will the quantitative values of these elements be established? The answer to the first of these is found in the indefinite number of ordinates that may be drawn perpendicularly from the axis of the *roulette* to points on its circumference. But, to pick up our second question, what will the values—the lengths—of these ordinates be? We must refer them to some known quantity or quantities. Here Pascal had the crucial intuition, and it resembles something we have seen before. Just as he found the way to solve problems of conic sections by introducing another figure, the *hexagramme mystique*, to which every conic section could be referred, so here he attacks the problem of the cycloid curve by referring it, reducing it even, to the circle that generates it. That circle, or half of it to be exact, functions as the heuristic principle. "Il paraît," he says, and he means not "it seems" but "it is clear": "Il paraît ... qu'on trouve la roulette entière dans son seul cercle générateur."[19] The consequence of this intuition is that the length of each ordinate to the *roulette* is equal (as to length) to the portion of that same ordinate that is enclosed in the generating half circle, plus a certain portion of the circumference of that half circle. With this equation a value for every ordinate in the roulette is established, and the summations called for in the analysis may be performed.

I realize that this account is schematic and perhaps obscure. Something like the following will suffice for our purposes: Pascal sees that what he wants to know can be found by executing an elaborate series of additions, of additions of lines; he sees further—and this is the crucial step—that values can be set for those lines by relating them to their equivalents in the generating circle; with the fixing of those values, the additive processes may be expressed so as to give the formulas for determining *dimensions* and *centres de gravité* in the desired cases.

Once Pascal has attained his results in one order, such as that of his figure taken as a flat surface, he shifts the inquiry to a new level, that of solids, by rotating parts of the surfaces on the axis and on the base, where measurement, addition, and balancing take place once more; and finally, he turns to similar calculations for the curved surfaces produced when the solids were generated.

Two other points merit attention here. Both underline features characteristic of geometrical procedure as Pascal understands it. The first flows immediately from what has just been said. It concerns the aspiration—inherent in this way of thinking—to put together sequences that move from simple beginnings to complex endings: thus the steady progression in the order of geometrical space from lines to plane surfaces to solids to surfaces on solids, or in the order of geometrical discourse the progressions from a few definitions and axioms to rich and coherent harvests of consequences. (Recall that Pascal discovered a proposition known in the seventeenth century as "la Pascale," from which, it is said, 400 other propositions could be derived.) My second and related point has to do with another constant aim of the geometrician—generalization, when what appears to be useful in a particular case can be shown to be universally applicable. At the beginning of the "Letter from M. Dettonville to M. de Carcavi," Pascal announces his intention of giving not only the solutions to the problems set for the contest, but also to show the methods used and how he arrived at them. Then, a few lines later "les méthodes" became "ma méthode," and he says:

Je ne me contenterai donc pas de vous donner les calculs, desquels voici celui du cas que j'avais proposé. . . . Mais je vous découvrirai de plus ma méthode générale pour les centres de gravité, qui vous plaîra d'autant plus qu'elle est plus universelle; car elle sert également à trouver les centres de gravité des plans, des solides, des surfaces courbes et des lignes courbes. (131)[20]

Such statements occur several times in this collection of papers. The one just cited generalizes on the theme of centers of gravity. Here is another that follows it up on the theme of the measurement of curved lines. It comes from the "letter from M. Dettonville to M. Huyghens":

Comme j'ai su que M. de Carcavi vous devait envoyer des problèmes que j'avais proposés touchant la *roulette*, je l'ai prié d'y joindre la dimension des courbes de toutes sortes de roulettes. ... Je n'ai qu'une seule méthode pour la dimension des lignes de toutes sortes de roulettes; en sorte que, soit qu'elles soient simples, allongées, ou raccourcies, ma construction est toujours pareille. ... (182)[21]

The process of demonstration, which takes place in the register of language, assumes into its account the elements, subdivisions, subtotals, equalities, and proportional relationship discernible in the figures. And that process is both fruitful—it multiplies consequences—and, when properly conceived, extendable, capable of being generalized so as to treat many or all of the categories that have some relation to the original problem.

My aim in the preceding pages is twofold: (1) to give by means of a brief report some insight into the content of the mathematical treatises; and (2) to analyze the habit of thought and language discernible in them. Without the first it is hard to convey the distinctive character of the second; and one must have the results of the second if one is to follow the developing complexity and unity of Pascal's thought. (I shall have more to say on this in chapter 5.) The geometrical method, though of course valid and proper in the problem areas of abstract number and space, is not strictly limited to them. It enters into or has an effect on other inquiries. It is applied in the investigation of natural phenomena, as we shall soon see, and it stands in an antithetical relation to the dialectical and rhetorical lines of reasoning that come to the fore in the *Pensées* and in the *Ecrits sur la grâce*. As intellectual techniques geometry, mathematical physics, dialectic, and rhetoric all have a place in Pascal's thought, and the correct working of each presupposes the existence and potentialities of the others.

Liquids and Balances

To understand Pascal's discoveries in the area of physics we must, once again, study an odd assortment of documents that vary in length and degrees of completion. First come the *Expériences nouvelles touchant le vide* (October 1647) and the correspondence arising out of them with Père Noël and with Le Pailleur (October–February 1647–48). Then we have the *Récit de la grande expérience*, the account of an experiment designed by Pascal but performed by Florin Périer on the Puy-de-Dôme (September 1648). It confirmed Pascal's

view that nature's supposed horror of a vacuum was a fiction. To
this dossier may be added the letters of July and August of 1651
to Ribeyre: they form in fact a kind of transition. Pascal wrote them
to defend himself—in connection with the *Expériences nouvelles*—
against insinuated charges that he had taken credit for Torricelli's
work. He also announced that he was finishing a "Traité du vide."
Apparently that was never completed, for all we have is a project of
the preface (though it is, nonetheless, an extremely important sketch,
and we shall return to it). The substance of the work alluded to is
perhaps included in the *Traités de l'équilibre des liqueurs et de la
pesanteur de l'air* [Treatises on the equilibrium of liquids and the
weight of air], published posthumously in 1663.

As always with Pascal, the beginning point is reality, things and
not ideas (or what would be even worse, figments of the imagination,
such as nature's supposed horror of a vacuum). However, instead of
the real quantities of arithmetic and geometry, we are now to study
physical bodies. To see the problem as Pascal saw it and to recover
some of the associations active in his mind, we need to recall two
basic factors in his dualism: nature is composed of bodies and souls
(or minds). Moving to a lower level, we must recognize the fact that
bodies are in these inquiries liquids or solids (Pascal works mainly
with the former). There was a similar but not exactly parallel distinction in the case of quantity: continuous versus discontinuous.

Here the concepts and devices drawn from geometry impinge radically on the realm of physics and determine what in fact we are to
know about bodies. I say that because when we describe them as
being either solid or liquid we are attending to their limits and
dimensions. To their limits, because solids and liquids are distinguished according as they have fixed or flexible boundaries; and to
their dimensions or measurable aspects in the sense that we are
interested solely in their mass and weight. The subject matter of
Pascal's physics is finite reality in certain of its geometrical and cal-
culable aspects. His is a purely quantitative approach: that is one
of the striking things that come out of the irreconcilable polemic with
Père Noël, who reasons from dogmas concerning earth, air, fire, and
water that are essentially qualitative.

All of these points become more specific when they are referred
to Torricelli's experiment with water and mercury. At the outset of
the *Expériences nouvelles* Pascal describes carefully what took place.

Il y a environ quatre ans qu'en Italie on éprouva qu'un tuyau de verre de quatre pieds, dont un bout est ouvert et l'autre est scellé hermétiquement, étant rempli de vif-argent, puis l'ouverture bouchée avec le doigt ou autrement, et le tuyau disposé perpendiculairement à l'horizon, l'ouverture bouchée étant vers le bas, et plongée de deux ou trois doigts dans l'autre vif-argent, contenu en un vaisseau moitié plein de vif-argent et l'autre moitié d'eau; si on débouche l'ouverture demeurant toujours enfoncée dans le vif-argent du vaisseau, le vif-argent du tuyau descend en partie, laissant au haut du tuyau un espace vide en apparence, le bas du même tuyau demeurant plein du même vif-argent jusqu'à une certaine hauteur. (195)[22]

How can the behavior of the mercury be explained? And what is in that apparently empty space?

It is instructive to contrast Pascal's attitude with that of his rival and critic, the Jesuit Noël. To do so gives us not only a clear sense of Pascal's intuitions, but also a glimpse of a fateful moment in the upheaval under way in seventeenth-century science. Noël sees things in terms of microcosm and macrocosm. The microcosm is the human body, filled to the brim with its four humors and their mixtures; and the macrocosm is the whole of nature filled, in turn, with the four elements and their mixtures. Since it is the "nature" of nature to be full, any attempt to empty a space in it meets with an aversion ready to exert an unlimited force to prevent a vacuum. And so, to return to Torricelli, that part of the tube that appears to be empty has air in it, rarefied air pushed through the pores of the glass.

Pascal could never accept these images and ideas. To him physical nature is not like a human being. It consists of bodies that are inanimate, that have not the slightest trace of soul or mind. Hence it cannot have desires or aversions. Noël conceives of space as a receptacle; to Pascal it is an absence—something between *néant* or nothingness and body; or to put the matter more positively, it is an unbounded milieu partly occupied by bodies and in which they may move. Space and bodies are perfectly matched in Noël's hypothesis; but Pascal thinks, obviously, that nature has more than enough space to accommodate the bodies in it.

If for Noël the basic tendency of nature is keeping a full receptacle full, for Pascal that tendency would seem to be movement toward rest. That means, specifically, that particular bodies move from an unstable to a stable state, and they do this by virtue of their weight.

They have weight, and for all practical purposes in Pascal's theory, they *are* weight. Now the movement of a weight is brought to rest by a counterweight. And there is the explanatory principle adopted by Pascal: an equilibrium that adjusts two weights to each other, the two weights being the column of mercury and the balancing column of air. Pascal completes the picture by adding the notion of proportional variation. This is necessary because the weights are not necessarily fixed. The weight of the air or air pressure varies in space according to the altitude of the observer and in time with changes in the weather; and the height of the mercury column varies in proportion. Pascal finds many uses for the notion of equilibrium. We have already encountered it in geometry, where it appeared in the search for centers of gravity in lines, planes, and solids. Here we see it transferred and adapted to an investigation where physical phenomena are being systematically measured. And anyone familiar with the theological and apologetic writings will recognize it as a principle used by Pascal in dealing with realities that have nothing to do with mathematics or physics: with grace (the truth consists in striking a balance between two exactly opposed doctrines), with man (he stands like a pivot between two infinites in nature), or with Jesus Christ (he is the center of both the Old and the New Testaments, and he combines both human and divine natures).

In the physical treatises and associated documents Pascal makes explicit from time to time several important points about intellectual method. For example, in his reply to the objections posed by Noël when the *Expériences nouvelles* first appeared, he makes an assertion, just after the opening civilities, that will regulate the whole debate: "permettez-moi de vous rapporter une règle universelle, qui s'applique à tous les sujets particuliers, où il s'agit de reconnaître la vérité."[23] The principle is accepted by all those who seek something "solide" and fully satisfying for the mind. We have met it already, but never before so clearly put or in language so authentically Pascalian. The rule may be broken down into two parts or phases:

c'est qu'on ne doit jamais porter un jugement décisif de la négative ou de l'affirmative d'une proposition, que ce que l'on affirme ou nie n'ait une de ces deux conditions: savoir, ou qu'il paraisse si clairement et si distinctement de soi-même aux sens ou à la raison, suivant qu'il est sujet à l'un ou à l'autre, que l'esprit n'ait aucun moyen de douter de sa certitude, et c'est ce que nous appelons *principes* ou *axiomes*; comme, par exemple,

si à choses égales on ajoute choses égales, les touts seront égaux. ...
(201)[24]

That is the first condition, the necessity for *évidence*, self-evidence,
direct and indubitable intuition, as the motivating force behind judgment. We shall come back later to the implications of the three related notions of "sens," "raison," and "esprit." Now follows the second
condition attached to what one affirms or denies:

ou qu'il se déduise par des conséquences infaillibles et nécessaires de tels
principes ou axiomes, de la certitude desquels dépend toute celle des conséquences qui en sont tirées; comme cette proposition, *les trois angles
d'un triangle sont égaux à deux angles droits*, qui n'étant pas visible d'elle-
même, est démontrée évidemment par des conséquences infaillibles de
tels axiomes. Tout ce qui a une de ces deux conditions est certain et
véritable, et tout ce qui n'en a aucune passe pour douteux et incertain.
(201)[25]

When stated this way, the two conditions have a power of negation,
a capacity to dispose peremptorily of many statements that otherwise
might pass as judgments, or in Pascal's words, "jugements décisifs."
These criteria make it easy to identify and to dismiss any "vision,"
"caprice," "fantaisie," "idée," or "belle pensée" (I reproduce his
graded list of possibilities) that has found its way into the discussion.

The breadth of Pascal's grasp of the whole subject, as he admin-
isters this little lesson in logic to the rector of the Collège de Clermont, appears at the end of the paragraph from which I have been
quoting: "Et nous réservons pour les mystères de la foi, que le Saint-
Esprit a lui-même révélés, cette soumission d'esprit qui porte notre
croyance à des mystères cachés aux sens et à la raison" (201).[26] In
the back of his mind when he treats one of the motivations of judgment one regularly finds a reference to the other: if he is pressing the
claims of *évidence* as available to sense and reason, he does not forget
that of revelation and inspiration, and vice versa.

The examples adduced by Pascal in the citations come from geometry, and as we have seen, arithmetic and geometry provide in the
realm of numbers and figures sequences that will be reflected in the
movement from antecedents to consequents that is characteristic of
demonstration. But numbers and figures are abstract and immaterial
(those are Pascal's adjectives), while the subject matter of physical

science is real bodies observable by sense in space and time. A
symptom of this important shift may be seen in the fact that the
couple *cause / effect* now emerges in the discussion: it would have
been implausible in a mathematical treatise. In studying natural
phenomena Pascal intends to bring principles and consequences expressed in statements into exact correlation with sequences that are
sought and established in things; and the latter are, properly speaking,
connections of cause and effect. Hence the new importance of sense-
experience—our link with the outside world—and its peculiar certi-
fying force; hence also the need for a new technique of discovery:
experimentation.

In geometry or mathematics in general Pascal knew that invention
and demonstration determine what is true and what is false. Each
is a separate gift, a distinct faculty, and happy is he who has both.
Actually, few have the "genium audax inventionis," even fewer the
"genium elegans demonstrationis" (101), and fewer still have the
combination of the two. But, as the context in which these phrases
occur seems to suggest, both are basically rational activities; they
parallel or address the special kind of reality that forms the subject
matter of arithmetic and geometry. Where, as in physics, truth must
consist of a harmony of thought (and language) on the one side and
perceptible things on the other, it is necessary to pay particular attention to sensation, to its vagaries, to the conditions under which
its findings may be trusted. In short, one must convert ordinary sensation into contrived and controlled observation—into experimentation.
And it will be the function of such observation to separate true from
false accounts. Pascal recognizes this discriminatory function in both
a negative and a positive way. We return to the idea of causes and
effects, since accounts or hypotheses presume to say why things happen as they do.

Car comme une même cause peut produire plusieurs effets différents, un
même effet peut être produit par plusieurs causes différentes. C'est ainsi
que, quand on discourt humainement du mouvement, de la stabilité de
la terre, tous les mouvements et rétrogadations des planètes s'ensuivent
parfaitement des hypothèses de *Ptolémée*, de *Tycho*, de *Copernic* et de
beaucoup d'autres qu'on peut faire, de toutes lesquelles une seule peut
être véritable. Mais qui osera faire un si grand discernement, et qui pourra,
sans danger d'erreur, soutenir l'une au préjudice des autres? (203)[27]

Curious sentence, which by the word "humainement" indicates cautiously the tension, unavoidable in the minds of many seventeenth-century thinkers, between biblical astronomy and the kind that men may formulate. Pascal is not interested in imagining experiments in this area. But hypotheses do at last have to meet the test of empirical verification, and Pascal has no doubt as to how those of Noël will fare.

Vous voyez par là qu'encore que de votre hypothèse s'ensuivissent tous les phénomènes de mes expériences elle serait de la nature des autres; et que, demeurant toujours dans les termes de la vraisemblance, elle n'arriverait jamais à ceux de la démonstration. Mais j'espère vous faire un jour voir plus au long, que de son affirmation s'ensuivent absolument les choses contraires aux expériences. (203)[28]

Although Pascal speaks here of experiments in the plural, and has in mind the series on which he reports in the *Expériences nouvelles*, we know that his trump card in the discussion was the so-called "Grande expérience," performed by his brother-in-law, Florin Périer, at successive elevations between Clermont-Ferrand and the top of the Puy-de-Dôme.

Two qualifications are needed if we are to appreciate what Pascal accomplished. In the first place, the hypothesis itself was not original with him: Torricelli is said to have suspected that the problematic behavior of the mercury in the tube was due to the weight of the column of air bearing down on the vessel into which the tube was submerged. In the second place, the general conception of the experiment needed to settle the matter was not original with Pascal, either. His contribution was to hit on the place and to set up the particular conditions under which the experiment could be performed in a precise and convincing way. To him goes the credit for the execution of the experiment (though Florin Périer was obviously a useful assistant).

The "grande expérience" is essentially a series of repetitions of what Torricelli had done. It was designed to show the co-variation of two factors observable in a balance situation (we find again, at the heart of the experiment, the leading principle mentioned earlier: the experimental method is simply a way of applying that principle to the subject matter). It comes down to changing the weight on one side of the balance and then observing what happens on the other.

In expressing qualifications regarding Pascal's originality I do not mean to belittle Pascal's accomplishment. Perhaps its nature is best grasped in the written accounts, in the "Récit de la grande expérience" and in the two posthumously published treatises on the equilibrium of liquids and on the weight of the atmosphere. One cannot help admiring the acute awareness of correct scientific procedure, the lucid control of the data, the principles, and the techniques of investigation relevant to the problem. Or the discerning sense of the validity of the results: Pascal did not allow himself, after the *Expériences nouvelles*, to call into question completely the *horror vacuï*, though he had established it as finite rather than infinite; the categorical denial came only after the experimental findings established an undoubtable case. Or the sense of logical sequence in setting out his results: the treatise on the weight of the atmosphere is a model in this regard. It lays down the principle of air pressure as a force exerted on all bodies, then lists the effects hitherto explained by nature's horror, then takes them up, one by one, with additions, showing that they may be explained by the weight of the air; then, after the series of chapters relating causes and effects in *simple* relations, it moves into problems where variations in the cause produces *proportional* variations in the effects; next Pascal broadens its scope to consider the heights attained by water in pumps in various locations (Paris, Clermont, Dieppe) and, with a virtuoso touch, concludes with a calculation of the weight of all the air surrounding the earth (8,283,889,440,000,000,000 *livres* or pounds). There is also something to admire, I think, in Pascal's intellectual courage. As he says in the note to the reader that closes the "Récit," "Le consentement universel des peuples et la foule des philosophes concourent à l'établissement de ce principe, que la nature souffrirait plutôt sa destruction propre, que le moindre espace vide."[29] In other words, he was not just addressing some technical mathematical demonstrations to a few friends and *savants*; he was correcting an error about nature that trained and untrained people had held for centuries. The *plenum* had to give way to the existence of the *vacuum*, the empty space in which bodies move in time-sequence. Instead of being a container that is always full, nature is an infinite space containing bodies having measurable relationships to each other. Although Pascal's experiments were performed on earth, in just a few places, and with essentially simple materials, they had implications of universal scope.

The Dividing Line

In some ways the fragmentary and incomplete preface to the projected treatise on the *vide* is the most valuable document in the collection of mathematical and physical works. It makes explicit the assumptions that underlie those treatises and, in addition, it opens up the possibility of serious inquiries in a very different domain. Pascal sets out to treat the question, how much respect is due the ancients? His opening sentence is syntactically incomplete, but the meaning comes across clearly:

Le respect que l'on porte à l'antiquité étant aujourd'hui à tel point, dans les matières où il doit avoir moins de force, que l'on se fait des oracles de toutes ses pensées, et des mystères même de ses obscurités; que l'on ne peut plus avancer de nouveautés sans péril, et que le texte d'un auteur suffit pour détruire les plus fortes raisons.... (23)[30]

He will avoid substituting one vice for another, extreme disrespect for extreme respect. But there is no need to accept blindly ancient views about certain subject matters, and specifically those that may be verified in direct experience and by reasoning. Armchair thinking with the books of the ancients in hand cannot take the place of questioning nature and observing its responses. The ancients may have been right, given the instruments they had to work with and the particular phenomena for which they were trying to account. But one cannot suspend for them the rules of *évidence* and of demonstrative reasoning. Moreover, it is of the nature of certain sciences—geometry, arithmetic, music, physics, medicine, architecture—to admit of increase, development, and progress. The ancients were in at the beginning, of course; and yet we are more ancient than they: and this leads Pascal to draw the famous image of mankind as having a history like that of a single man's life-cycle.

De sorte que toute la suite des hommes, pendant le cours de tous les siècles, doit être considérée comme un même homme qui subsiste toujours et qui apprend continuellement: d'où l'on voit avec combien d'injustice nous respectons l'antiquité dans ses philosophes; car, comme la vieillesse est l'âge le plus distant de l'enfance, qui ne voit que la vieillesse dans cet homme universel ne doit pas être cherchée dans les temps proches de sa naissance, mais dans ceux qui en sont les plus éloignés? (232)[31]

To return, however, to the idea of a balance: Pascal does not simply jettison one side of an important and fruitful distinction. He sees an important situation, often encountered, where respect for the ancients and for authority is due. That situation obtains where you cannot, by the nature of things, see for yourself, where you have no alternative but to take someone else's word for what was or is the case. Certain disciplines depend solely, he says, on memory (as opposed to sense and reason). This leads to a separation of the sciences into two categories, historical and dogmatic.

Il faut considérer que les unes [matières] dépendent seulement de la mémoire et sont purement historiques, n'ayant pour objet que de savoir ce que les auteurs ont écrit; les autres dépendent seulement du raisonnement, et sont entièrement dogmatiques, ayant pour objet de chercher et découvrir les vérités cachées. (230)[32]

What are these historical subjects? History, of course, and then geography, jurisprudence, languages, and theology. In these sciences, according to Pascal, we learn and accept as true what properly established authorities say.

The status of theology is a special one. One must have recourse to authority, as I said above, to know in those areas where we cannot use our own knowing powers. If history is involved, or the geography of distant countries, it is physically impossible for us to know directly and immediately, though in theory we could know if we were present at the time or in the place in question. However, in theological matters, where the objects of knowledge exceed by their nature the grasp of our powers, we have no possible way of knowing except by authority.

Mais où cette autorité a sa principale force, c'est dans la théologie, parce qu'elle y est inséparable de la vérité, et que nous ne la connaissons que par elle: de sorte que pour donner la certitude entière des matières les plus incompréhensibles de la nature, il suffit de les faire voir dans les livres sacrés (comme pour montrer l'incertitude des choses les plus vraisemblables, il faut seulement faire voir qu'elles n'y sont pas comprises)....
(230)[33]

This pleading in favor of reason that goes hand in hand with a valorizing of authority brings us suddenly to a kind of summit and to a broad view, in which all of Pascal's intellectual and artistic undertakings find their places. To this point we have been following Pascal's work on subject matters that come under the jurisdiction of reason—of reason alone in geometry and arithmetic, or reason supplemented by sense in the sciences of natural phenomena. But the *Lettres provinciales* and the *Pensées*, to be examined in the next two chapters of this book, take us decidedly into the sphere where authority is supreme.

A word of caution, however. On neither side of this watershed are we justified in proceeding as though Pascal separated rigorously and exclusively the two realms of reason and authority. That is not true, even in his scientific work where (it is plain) he attaches a great deal of importance to the opinions of his peers among contemporary mathematicians and physicists, to say nothing of the enthusiastic esteem in which he holds that great ancient, Archimedes. It is certainly not true in works like the *Provinciales* and the *Pensées*, where authority may give answers to the great questions but reason still has an enormous role to play in the tasks of discerning truth, communicating it, and developing its consequences.

Chapter Three

The *Provinciales*

Arnauld and the Meanings of "Grace" (Letters 1–3)

The *Lettres provinciales* (or *Provinciales*, as they are called on the title page of the first edition) came out of a period of concentrated activity and effort that Pascal undertook in behalf of his friends at Port-Royal. An indication of the chronological limits of the period is given by the publication dates of the letters, which appeared at more or less regular intervals from the end of January 1656 to the end of March 1657. In all Pascal composed eighteen letters; a nineteenth was projected and partly written, but then abandoned as the polemic continued in another form and under different auspices.

The series begins with a letter designed to defend, before as wide an audience as possible, that indefatigable spokesman for the Jansenist point of view, Antoine Arnauld, who was about to be censured by the theologians of the Sorbonne. Succeeding letters deal at length with the moral principles of the Jesuits, their "maximes" as they are expressed in the books of casuistry and also in their other books and pamphlets. The series ends with two letters that return to doctrinal issues concerning grace that were raised in the very first letter, though Pascal now treats them in quite general terms, without limiting his arguments to the case of an individual. (Arnauld's condemnation occurred in the interval between the third and fourth letters, and the range of the discussion broadened from that point.) The best procedure is, I think, to take up each letter in turn, to follow in it the course of the argument and the evolution of the rhetorical framework that Pascal invented for it, and then, in a concluding section to return to some of the main themes for a fuller discussion and for comments on Pascal's way of working them out.

Letter 1 (23 January 1656). A coalition of *docteurs* in the Sorbonne have attacked Arnauld for the stand he has taken on five propositions declared to be heretical by the pope and alleged to be found in the *Augustinus* of Jansenius. Arnauld denies that the propo-

50

sitions are in the book (the *question de fait*, the question of fact), but at the same time, he condemns them, *if* they are there (the *question de droit*, the question of right or truth). The contention centers on the workings of divine grace in human conduct. In the letter representatives of the various points of view have their say. It becomes clear that the difficulties are more apparent and verbal than real and substantial. But the conflicts remain at the end, because the forces arrayed against Arnauld are much less interested in grace than in discrediting him.

Pascal did not invent the theology that underlies the argument of the letter, but he did invent the rhetorical framework in which it is conveyed. The letter proceeds on two levels: (1) that of a communication sent by the writer to a "provincial de ses amis," and (2) that of an investigation, in which the writer seeks out spokesmen for the opposed views in the controversy. What takes place on the second level becomes the substance of what is transmitted on the first. The situation on the first level is uncomplicated—only two people are involved in a one-way event; it is less simple in the second aspect. The writer goes to M. N., a "docteur de Navarre," and then to another M. N., who is a friend of the writer; this M. N. takes him to a Jansenist; after a conversation with the Jansenist the writer returns to the "docteur"; then he goes back to the Jansenist, who refers him to a disciple of Le Moyne and to a disciple of Nicolai; he visits and talks with the former; later, while he is with the latter, the conversation is interrupted by the arrival of the disciple of Le Moyne, and the investigation ends at that point.

What is going on in all this activity and talk? It is plain that Pascal has made a number of important technical choices. The writer wants to explain to his friend (and to all readers of the letter) the disagreements in the Sorbonne. However, instead of a piece of expository prose he imagines a *narrative* that turns into a series of *dialogues*, and the crucial parts in the dialogues are spoken by characters who have taken on roles in a *drama*, an action intended to produce a vote in the Sorbonne against Arnauld and a declaration that his views on grace are heretical. The frame of reference found in this letter, which involves the writer, his friend, and five others, four of whom are actively engaged in the polemic, is the most complex to be seen in all the *Provinciales*. Thereafter and progressively Pascal simplifies things. It is interesting to watch him strip away the elements of his dramatizing technique, to the point of eliminating entirely the fictive characters. But from the first letter he has shown the intimate association of ideas with men and their motives. He never gives that up: in fact, one of the great scandals for him in the controversy arises from the realization that doctrine is being overthrown by political designs, that the terms and propositions of arguments have become instruments not for thinking correctly about theological questions and for producing agreement but for widening the influence of the Society of Jesus.

Letter 2 (29 January 1656). The defense of Arnauld continues. Two points are in dispute, on the subjects of *pouvoir prochain* and *grâce suffisante.*[1] Pascal dealt with the first in letter 1; he now proceeds to the second. The contention turns on the opposition between *grâce suffisante*, invented by modern theologians (Molina, in particular), who lack authority, and *grâce efficace*, presented by Pascal as orthodox and founded on beliefs going back to the biblical patriarchs. An important fact comes to light: the alliance between the Jesuits and the new Thomists on the side of *grâce suffisante* is not the result of doctrinal agreement. The *Jacobins/Thomistes* actually have a tradition of upholding the notion of *grâce efficace*, and therefore agree with the Jansenists. On orders from their superiors they pretend to be in accord with the Jesuits. And so, as in the first letter, the basic line of thought runs from an attempt made by the inquiring writer to clarify a theological difficulty in proper terms to the recognition on his part that the real issue is power and prestige. "Grâce suffisante" and "pouvoir prochain" are nothing more than rallying cries.

The framework of this letter, considerably less complex than that of letter 1, is formed by a series of meetings and conversations among four people. The writer of the letter tells the "provincial" of visits to M. N., "notre ancien ami," and then to a Jacobin, where he finds a Jansenist present also. The ensuing three-sided discussion confirms what M. N. had said.

Letter 3 (9 February 1656). Published as a preface to this letter we have the one and only communication from the fictive addressee of the series. This "Réponse du provincial aux deux premières lettres de son ami" assures the writer that everyone reads, understands, and believes the two letters. The first has, in fact, received the approval both of a member of the Academy and of a distinguished lady (who may have been Mlle de Scudéry). Letter 3 was composed after the censure of Arnauld had been voted in the Sorbonne. The writer argues that the proposition serving as the basis of the discussion and vote is so obviously in harmony with doctrine formally expressed by the church fathers that ordinary readers are unable to see in what the heresy consists. This paradoxical situation leads him to consult a doctor of the Sorbonne who is informed and neutral. The doctor states at once that the opponents of Arnauld have no case. But they have the necessary votes, and the condemnation, once proclaimed, will stick in people's minds and have its effect. The writer concludes that this is a new kind of heresy, falling not on Arnauld's theology but on his person, so that to cease to be heretical he has no choice but to cease to be, purely and simply.

This letter contains almost no dialogue; it has been replaced by the writer's long introductory statement and by the similarly long explanation given by the informant. Pascal's view of the rhetorical framework appropriate to what he wants to do is clearly evolving.

The Jesuits' Moral Principles (Letters 4–10)

Letter 4 (25 February 1656). Pascal now leaves the case of Arnauld and moves from a defensive to a clearly offensive posture. He treats on a general level some questions to be examined in detail in letters 6–10, where the *maximes* or principles of Jesuit morality are studied. In the present letter he asks, in effect, under what conditions may an action be counted as sinful, "imputée à péché"? Once again the Jansenists and the Jesuits are at odds. The latter invoke the principle of *grâce actuelle*, a divine inspiration that comes just before an act is to be committed. If it is not present, if the will of God is not consciously related to that act and to those circumstances, no sin may be imputed. This notion makes no provision for sins that take us by surprise or for sins committed by hardened and habitual sinners. The Jesuit father who explains *grâce actuelle* is asked to show on what basis he advances it, and to cite his authorities. They all turn out to be Jesuits: Beauny, Annat, Le Moyne. Their argument fails when tried against the test of simple good sense and of passages taken from the Old and New Testaments. The Jesuit father brings in a short quotation from the *Ethics* of Aristotle to bolster his case, but it backfires. The context of the statement supports a view of voluntary action much closer to that of the Jansenists than to that of the Jesuits.

As a piece of composition and argument this letter is a masterpiece. The *dramatis personae* are the writer, his Jansenist friend, and the Jesuit father. Pascal defines the three roles, suggests character traits, and varies the tone from section to section—all with the hand of one who is in perfect control of the situation. He sets out and articulates the reasoning so that the pressure on the Jesuit increases steadily as he runs through his authorities, and then is obliged to face formidable objections from the Old Testament, from St. Paul, and from the words of Christ himself. The quotation from pagan Aristotle, on whom the Jesuit pinned his final hope, has the opposite effect and completes his rout.

Letter 5 (20 March 1656). Now Pascal begins to develop the general features of the moral theory taught and used by the "bons pères jésuites." They take as their first principle the conviction that it is useful and even necessary for the good of religion that their influence be extended everywhere, and that they should, in fact, govern all consciences. This enterprise requires that they have guidelines or maxims for everybody. And so the Jesuit casuists (taken collectively) provide rules for both rigorous Christians and lax Christians. Clearly, as Pascal and his inquirer state the case, they work in such a way that the client is always right. They do not aim to corrupt morals, but neither do they have as their unique aim to reform them.

The basis and A B C of their moral system is the doctrine of "probable opinions." The opinions in question are the rules for the guidance of Christians as they go about the practice of their religion, and, in particular, as they face their confessors or spiritual directors regarding actions that are or seem to be sinful. According to Escobar, one of the most famous of the Spanish casuists, an opinion is called probable when it is based on reasons that have a certain weight ("raisons de quelque considération," as Pascal translates the Latin text). Thence it happens sometimes that a single doctor, if he is quite serious, may render an opinion "probable." A confessor may then excuse acts that involve or appear to involve infractions of the commandments or the will of God on the basis of opinions made current by Escobar and his followers. To the inquirer who is writing the *Lettres provinciales* this seems to effect a fatal substitution: instead of going by principles drawn from the Bible, the fathers, and councils, and the declarations of popes, those who use the casuists' book are depending on a group of modern experts; they are substituting human for divine authority.

Three characters or persons appear on the scene as the letter develops: the writer-inquirer as usual, the well-informed friend (presumably M. N.), and the ingenuous *père jésuite.* The visit to the friend brings on the distinction of the Jesuits into two types: those who adopt a rigorous and evangelical view of morality and those who move in the direction of laxism, of making it easy for Christians to be so. There is little dialogue here, little that is dramatic; it is essentially a piece of exposition. On the other hand, the visit to the Jesuit father—who belongs to the second of the two types—turns into a lively discussion in which the writer learns a great deal and reacts strongly to what he learns. The father talks and acts exactly according to type, and so the exposition set down in the first visit is perfectly exemplified in the second. Moreover, Pascal whets our curiosity for the next instalment or episode by promising to show in the next letter how the casuists go about removing the contradictions between their teaching and that of Scripture and tradition.

Letter 6 (10 April 1656). It is worth noting that the miracle of the *Sainte-Epine* occurred on 25 March, in the interval between letters 5 and 6. This event must surely have encouraged Pascal and his collaborators to continue along the way they had begun in the polemic with the Jesuits. Letter 6 picks up immediately the thread of the discussion at the point where it had ended in the preceding letter. One after another, in order of increasing difficulty, the *père jésuite* deals with problems arising when the principles of the casuists appear to conflict with orthodox doctrine. Difficulties are resolved, first, by interpretation: that involves finding some favorable shade of meaning in a crucial term, which, if taken in its original sense, would defeat the casuist. Or again, by something called the "remarque des circonstances favorables": there one adduces attenuating circumstances not foreseen in statements prohibiting certain acts. And finally, by the doctrine of "double probability": here, since any opinion is only probable, arguments can be found for the opposing view, with the consequence that the Christian in doubt may, with a clear conscience, follow the one that is more to his liking. Principles like these and the attitude that underlies them, when applied to a catalog of all the vices that men in their corrupt state fall into, lead to a code where something appealing may be found for everybody in every case or extremity. And so it is natural for the writer and the Jesuit father to turn to the different classes of society and to discuss problems in the clergy, the nobility, and the third estate.

Pascal casts this letter in a format somewhat simpler than that of the preceding one. Only two people are present. The dialogue resembles in tone and movement what we saw in letter 5, though a nice bit of dramatic excitement is worked in at the end. When the writer points to a glaring case of inconsistency in the conduct of the Jesuits themselves, the *père*, incensed, threatens to break off the conversations if his interlocutor gives him any more such trouble.

Letter 7 (25 April 1656).   Direction of intention is a doctrine almost as important as that of probable opinions. The idea is to purify the intention where you cannot prevent the action. If someone harms someone else, the action may be excused by referring it to the intention of accomplishing some good. If one sins purely for the sake of sinning (surely a rare occurrence), the case is hopeless; but other cases may be adjusted. The power of the principle shines forth especially in cases concerning honor (we are now dealing with the nobility, after studying some abuses found in the clergy in letter 6). The desire for vengeance leads to duels and homicides, to the open breach of the commandment, Thou shalt not kill. However, the act of dueling may be justified if the intention of the duelist is not to kill but to defend a good, namely, his honor; and the vice of the means is corrected by the purity of the end. The discussion moves from one paradox to another as less and less significant offenses are seen to be occasions for possible and excusable homicide. Members of the clergy may kill not only to defend their lives, but also their property or the property of their order. The Jesuit Caramuel has even raised the question, whether Jesuits may kill Jansenists. The answer is no, because the Jansenists are only contributing—albeit against their wishes—to the *éclat* of the Society of Jesus. The writer points out that this is slender security: the Jansenists would become eligible for killing if a probable opinion judged them to be harming in fact the reputation of the Society.

The framework and presentation here is exactly the same as that in letter 6. Here, as before, one is struck by the way Pascal arranges carefully the steps in the argument, which rises by a beautifully controlled gradation to the quotation from Caramuel.

Letter 8 (28 May 1656).   The thought of the previous discussion is resumed after a prefatory paragraph: we are still going through the gamut of social distinctions and studying moral questions associated with people occupying those ranks. Having dealt with the clergy and with nobles (and valets) in letter 7, Pascal now takes up cases concerning judges, tradesmen, bankrupts, and thieves. The result is always the same: some way is found to excuse examples of bribery, usury, failure to live up to the law and to make restitution for damages or for harm done. At the end of this letter, which completes the broad picture of laxism as it applies to society, the writer presents in a transitional passage the promise of the *bon père* for future conversations. It now remains for the "provincial" and others to see what facilities the casuists have found for making devotion and salvation comfortable and easy. The previous instruction was specified according to social status, but in the next letters everyone is concerned, regardless of class; and taken together, the two parts will present a complete view of the *morale jésuite.*

The rhetorical frame is still that of the writer-inquirer and the Jesuit father engaged in conversation. Two points are worthy of note, however. For one thing the opening paragraph of the letter evokes not only the *provincial* but also other readers who are asking questions about the identity of the writer: is he a *docteur* of the Sorbonne? Is he one of four or five other people who are neither priests nor members of religious orders? Once before, in the "Réponse du provincial" inserted between the second and third letters, reference was made to a general audience, to the real audience for which Pascal was writing. In the second place, we see at more than one place in the letter indications of a coming change in the posture of the writer. He reports that he must restrain himself in his reactions to what he hears, so as not to shock the Jesuit father, and yet his astonishment and indignation make it harder and harder for him to keep still. He suggests that after satisfying his friend's curiosity about the new moral teaching he may feel obliged to make an open attack on it. This statement, put in tentative language, foreshadows the change in format to come in letter 11.

Letter 9 (3 July 1656). The letter describes at first a series of easy devotions that are, nonetheless, guaranteed to effect salvation, such as saying *bonjour* regularly to the Virgin Mary or having always a rosary in one's pocket. Next, since the *gens du monde* do not care for self-control or austerity, comes a group of vices—ambition, envy, vanity, avarice, *gourmandise*—that are so reconceived and redefined that no one is ever likely to fall into them. Then, as regards social relationships and especially intrigues between men and women, it is shown that by devices such as equivocation and mental restriction one may do very nearly what one pleases. Finally, we learn that there are ways of attending mass (with the attendant benefits) that require little concentration, seriousness, or even time. Pascal is developing, obviously, his principal thesis, that the Jesuits practice (if I may use a phrase he defines elsewhere in discussing persuasion) an *art d'agréer*, a style of morality designed to please, to win friends and influence, rather than to convert. Perhaps the perfect expression comes in the quotation from a manual written by Sanchez: "Il est permis à l'appétit naturel de jouir des actions qui lui sont propres"[2]—a principle that leaves little or nothing for grace to do. To the closing objection of the writer that this moral approach will alienate at least some serious Christians, the intrepid *père* replies that the Society cannot limit its appeal to such people; its profound intention is to adapt itself to all conditions of men. He looks forward to the next conversation, when the subject will be some novelties concerning penitence.

There is no change in the situation from that of letter 8: the exposition is fueled by quotations from books of casuistry, put forward by the Jesuit father. What is new is the gravity of the things discussed, and this leads to a heightened form of what we have seen before: the contrast between the perspective of the father, who relates enthusiastically what he deems to be authoritative solutions to moral problems, and that of the inquiring writer, who discerns in what he hears facile and arbitrary enormities.

Letter 10 (2 August 1656).   From the beginning of this letter we sense the coming of a climactic moment in the discussion with the *père*. This is so because of the logic behind the argument as Pascal articulates it. To him Christian morality in its practical effects flows from a distinction, clearly recognizable, between acts permitted and acts forbidden. By the reasonings of the casuists many things that were once forbidden are now permissible: that has in fact been the thesis of the preceding five letters. But, in spite of everything, in spite of all the facilities invented by the Jesuits, a few sins will remain unexcused, and the sinners will have to make their confessions and do their penances. The end of Christian morality will be at hand if the burden of these obligations can by some means be lifted.

Pascal thinks, of course, that the way has been prepared for that very thing to happen. As is usual with him, the statement of the case proceeds in a quite orderly fashion. There are six painful aspects in confession: shame at having committed the act or acts, recall of the circumstances, penance to be done, resolution not to repeat the offense, avoidance of occasions to sin, and regret. He takes up each of these in turn, with citations to show how every phase of the process has been undermined. It seems at last that even the commandment to love God ("the great commandment that includes the law and the prophets") may be dispensed with: it suffices that one not *hate* him, while keeping the other commandments. This is the last straw. In a passionate outburst the writer tells the priest that he and those he represents are overturning completely the law and the word of God, that they are accomplishing the very mystery of iniquity; and he prays that their eyes may be opened to the falsity of their principles. After other remarks in the same vein, he breaks off the conversations, and in view of the way they have gone, sees no likelihood of renewing them.

The end of this letter signals the end of the convention—basically rhetorical, but including something like a dramatic scenario—whereby an inquiring writer seeks out for the sake of an uninformed friend a Jesuit father for enlightenment on the subject of the Jesuit moral theory. An explosive denouement had become inevitable; the dialogue had reached the point of highest tension between the two points of view; and the distinctive traits of the two characters had become so pronounced that the deadlock was personal as well as intellectual. Moreover, Pascal reverses their roles at the end of the letter: the learner, the one normally spoken to, turns on his informant with a stream of apostolic eloquence. A new framework must be invented if the letters are to continue.

Replies to Criticisms and Attacks (Letters 11–16)

Letter 11 (18 August 1656). This letter is addressed not to the provincial friend but directly to the "révérends pères jésuites." It responds to attacks that have been published in protest against the preceding letters. The author of those letters, the accusation runs, has held sacred matters up to ridicule. Pascal makes at once a distinction between truths that the Spirit of God has revealed and errors that the spirit of man sets up in opposition. The former are "lovable" and "venerable" (two adjectives destined, incidentally, to play an important part in the *Pensées*); the latter are fair game and there is nothing unusual or wrong in ridiculing them. Pascal draws up an impressive list of precedents, beginning with God himself, who remarked, according to the book of Genesis, "Ecce Adam quasi unus ex nobis."[3] Prophets, Jesus Christ, the fathers, St. Augustine have all on occasion taken to *raillerie* in the presence of error. Of course some rules must be observed: one must tell the truth, use discretion, treat errors only in this style, and always write in a spirit of charity. Pascal takes his opponents to task for not observing these principles but defends what he has done as consistent with them. Indeed, how else could one deal with those books of casuistry if not with laughter? One's surprise on reading their opinions provokes that reaction—and here we get in passing Pascal's formula for the essence of the comic: "il est impossible que cette surprise ne fasse rire, parce que rien n'y porte davantage qu'une disproportion surprenante entre ce qu'on attend et ce qu'on voit."[4] Again, as Tertullian says (another precedent), to treat such things seriously is to authorize them.

Letter 11 effects a great change in the circumstances and shape of the controversy. It takes on new layers of concern: until now there have been two subjects—what the Jesuits are saying and doing, and what Pascal reports them as saying and doing; to those are now added what they say about his accounts of their behavior and what he proposes in reply and refutation. From *reportage* (not exactly objective, it is true) based on imagined visits and conversations Pascal finds himself moving into direct encounter and debate, with a corresponding rise in the intensity of the polemic tone. Long-contained indignation is now loosed; one senses a certain enthusiasm for the combat, now open at last. He adapts to his purposes with slight changes a text from Tertullian (I italicize the words taken without change from the source):

Ne trouvez-vous pas, mes Pères, que ce passage est bien juste à notre sujet? Les lettres que j'ai faites jusqu'ici ne sont qu'*un jeu avant un véritable combat*. Je n'ai fait encore que me jouer, *et vous montrer plutôt les blessures qu'on vous peut faire que je ne vous en ai fait*. (420)[5]

The whole affair is snowballing; the stakes are higher than ever; and both parties are bloodthirsty.

Letter 12 (9 September 1656). Pascal says that he had intended to answer next in the letters the question of why the Jesuits had engaged in slanderous attacks on him. But they have charged *him* with slander and deception in misrepresenting their doctrines. They are now accusing him of what they (as he interprets their words and actions) have been doing to him. And since their charges bear on specific points concerning simony and alms-giving, Pascal replies on those points, showing by citations that his report on their "maxims" was correct. Although this deflects him from the direction he intended to take, it gives him another opportunity to return to their moral theory and to enlarge on his earlier analyses. In their criticisms they can only resort to Scholastic jargon and other evasions, while he deals with questions of fact, with particular terms and statements, and with the conclusions to which they give rise.

Indirectly, however, he is able to advance the argument as he had wished. He states once more the overriding aim of his opponents: "to maintain the prestige and glory of their order." They use that purpose to legitimize any means that is effective, even slander; they subvert thus the proper order of things, granting to men what they desire and giving to God words and appearances. Or, more precisely and in more usual Pascalian language: the Jesuits are trying to settle issues that belong in one order with means drawn from another. A strange conflict results.

C'est une étrange et longue guerre que celle où la violence essaie d'opprimer la vérité. Tous les efforts de la violence ne peuvent affaiblir la vérité, et ne servent qu'à la relever davantage. Toutes les lumières de la vérité ne peuvent rien pour arrêter la violence, et ne font que l'irriter encore plus. (429) [6]

But the struggle is not equal or unending. God puts a limit to the course of violence, and truth eventually triumphs, for like God himself it is bound to subsist eternally.

Pascal continues to develop in this letter the possibilities inherent in his new rhetorical posture, by which, in the person of an unidentified author, he addresses the Jesuit fathers to their faces, and instead of writing reports about them—as in letters 1–10—enters into personal and doctrinal combat with them.

Letter 13 (30 September 1656). Pascal continues to defend himself against the accusation of *imposture*, of having misstated Jesuit doctrine on a number of specific points. Having replied in connection with simony and alms-giving in letter 12, he takes up the subject of homicide. From the books of casuistry he cites and collates passages tending to show that some Jesuits do approve of homicide for trivial offenses like a slap or evil speaking. These are, Pascal points out, matters of fact, *questions de fait*, that can be settled by opening one's eyes and looking at what is on the printed page.

Some casuists say that homicide is justifiable in theory, but it should not be encouraged in practice. Why not? Because large numbers of killings would do harm to the interests of the state. Pascal demolishes that as reasoning based on a reversal of orders: God's justice and his command, "Thou shalt not kill," come surely before human justice and the interests of the state. But, in the next place, how could such a maxim ever be thought of as having acceptable grounds? Pascal sees the key in the technique of probable opinions. What the Jesuit authorities say is *ipso facto* probable and satisfies the demands of conscience. That is the premise controlling the argument; then, if the thesis is advanced by some doctors—that homicide is justifiable—the conclusion inevitably follows, and the principle is established. The logical crudeness of the process tends to pass unnoticed because it occurs gradually. An opinion is expressed; picked up and repeated, it gains some currency; soon it has something like the force of custom, and the transition from speculation to practice becomes easy. Human decisions come in time to replace divine decrees. The fact that some casuists may take a different stand on the question does not matter: we are, after all, in the domain of the merely probable. On any issue, then, there may be a defensible *yes* and a defensible *no* as to what should be done—and one takes one's choice.

Several times in the letter Pascal refers to the theme of the Jesuits' opportunistic policy, which is set directly or indirectly against the theme of truth (this opposition is, in fact, one of the constants in the *Provinciales*). They make statements and advance arguments; they appear to be working on the level of doctrine; but in reality the influence and prosperity of the Company come first. That ordering of ends leads its members to give to those whose spiritual lives they direct facile, undemanding answers to moral questions, answers that offer two ways to moral safety instead of the simple and single way of the Holy Spirit. Letter 13 ends with an exclamation from Ecclesiastes: "Vae duplici corde, et ingredienti duabus viis."[7] Here as elsewhere in the *Provinciales* Pascal exercises his talent for vehement perorations and strong endings.

Letter 14 (23 October 1656).   Having given evidence for the "permission to kill" as one of the Jesuit principles, Pascal is ready to develop a great antithesis. Against his opponents he arrays a battery of authorities: God himself in the Decalogue, St. Paul, St. Chrysostom, St. Augustine, church law, and even the pagan Romans, who with their notions of natural and civil law were sounder than the Jesuits. How can Lessius, Molina, Escobar, Reginaldus, Filiutius, Baldellus, and other Jesuits prevail in such company? God alone has the authority that the excusers of homicide have taken upon themselves. He may and does delegate it to civil ministers, but the exercise of this awesome power is limited by many restrictions.

Becoming more specific, Pascal launches into a fresh antithesis, this time between civil procedure and the "justice" dealt out by the duelist defending his honor. In a civil case involving the death penalty there must be seven judges; none of them may have been offended or harmed by the defendant; the trial must take place during morning hours when minds are purer; it proceeds on the basis of sworn testimony interpreted in the light of the law; if the verdict is guilty, the condemned man is granted time to look to his conscience; and no judge who takes part in such a case may ever thereafter become a member of a holy order. Against all this due process, the person whose honor has been offended by a slap is, in the view of the casuists, entitled to be interested party, judge, and executioner in his own case, acting with no concern for the soul or state of conscience of his victim and incurring no penalty for his violence. That the Jesuits should put themselves in such a position seems to Pascal incomprehensible. If not for religion's sake, then for the sake of their own ends, which give priority to the standing of their order, they should condemn openly and voluntarily such inhuman opinions. In a more straightforward vein, to excite their horror, he recalls to them the story of Cain and Abel, the first homicide, and then the crucifixion of the *chef des justes*, the most righteous one of all, affirming finally that homicide is the sole crime that envelops everything in the destruction it wreaks: state, church, nature, and piety.

A long summarizing passage begins:

Il est permis, disent Lessius, Molina, Escobar, Reginaldus, Filiutius, Baldellus, et autres jésuites, *de tuer celui qui veut nous donner un soufflet.* Est-ce là le langage de Jésus-Christ? Répondez-nous encore. Serait-on sans honneur en souffrant un soufflet sans tuer celui qui l'a donné? *N'est-il pas véritable*, dit Escobar, que, tandis qu'un *homme laisse vivre celui qui lui a donné un soufflet, il demeure sans honneur?* Oui, mes Pères, *sans cet honneur* que le diable a transmis de son esprit superbe en celui de ses superbes enfants.... (440)[8]

The tone and character of the passage mark, if not a turn in the rhetorical situation, at least a change in the underlying imagery. We are now engaged less in a polemic or *battle* than in something like a public *trial*. After making his case in the strongest possible terms, Pascal summons his adversaries to answer specific questions. Of course he believes that no valid reply is possible: his aim is to *confondre*, to confound his opponents, to force a recognition of error, and to bring about a new course of action. We have the impression of being present at a face-to-face encounter in some courtroom.

Letter 15 (25 November 1656). Pascal turns now to a topic announced earlier: the way the Jesuits remove slander from the category of crimes and make no scruple of using it against their enemies, and in particular against the Jansenists. How should one meet the accusations of impiety and heresy made against them? Pascal's strategy is not to assert facts in reply, not to become lost in details. Instead he resorts to a formidable *ad hominem* argument: their acts of slander are not accidents; they do not come out of ignorance or misapprehension; they reflect convictions and matters of principle. For the Jesuits have redefined calumny. Taking it out of its biblical context—where the Decalogue forbids it expressly—they have changed it, through their technique of justification by probable opinions, into a means that may be used in defending one's honor. It thus becomes a venial sin only, and even that degree of fault is quickly forgotten.

Here Pascal reveals, he says with great emphasis, a *mystère* or secret of Jesuit tactics, and by revealing it he intends to destroy the credibility of his opponents. The mystery is in fact something very simple: they measure the virtue and faith of men by the regard men have for their society. Anyone who criticizes them soon finds himself declared a heretic: "c'est blesser l'honneur de l'Eglise que de blesser celui de votre société."[9] Unfortunately for them and fortunately for the truth, their method draws them into contradictions that undermine their arguments and give their intentions away. They assert both the *pour* and the *contre*, the *pro* and the *con*, in questions of morality (since they declare the same act by turns to be impious and free of wrong) and in questions of fact (since in repeated instances they have both denied and admitted the presence of disputed statements in books written by members of their order). Having in mind their self-serving ambiguities and their willingness to slander those who dare to oppose them, Pascal charges the Jesuit fathers with impudent lying: *Mentiris impudentissime*. This challenge, he asserts, is based on attested instances and is therefore unanswerable; or, if they attempt to make a reply, they prove their guilt. In conclusion he promises more of the same kind of indictment in defense of the innocent people who have been called impostors and heretics.

This letter increases the tension—though one would hardly have thought that possible—between Pascal and the *révérends pères*. Their campaign against him and his friends has collapsed. One important leitmotiv in the *Lettres provinciales*, the unscrupulous politics of the Jesuits, has emerged with even greater clarity than before. The laxism of their moral doctrine, which is designed to excuse the shortcomings of others, extends into the area of their own activities, where misrepresenting the characters and motives of others is an acceptable way of advancing their cause. The repeated use of the word *confondre* as an indication of Pascal's aim shows that a crisis is approaching in the conflict: one of the parties is to be reduced to silence or to an effort of self-defense that can only be self-incriminating.

Letter 16 (4 December 1656). Pascal considers in this letter slanderous accusations that have been directed toward certain ecclesiastics and religious, and specifically Saint-Cyran, Arnauld, and the nuns of Port-Royal. Letter 16 is longer by about one half than the preceding letters. For one thing, the charges treated by Pascal do not form a neat or brief list; and for another, this disparate agenda had to be dealt with quickly. There are hints in the letter and other evidence to suggest that Pascal and his friends feared the possibility of legal intervention that would have stopped all attacks on the Jesuits. In a note placed at the end of letter 16 (and still addressed to the Jesuit fathers) Pascal says, "Je n'ai fait celle-ci [cette lettre-ci] plus longue que parce que je n'ai pas eu le loisir de la faire plus courte" (453).[10] This paradoxical remark says much, in passing, about the ideal that guided Pascal in composition and expression.

The main points of doctrine in the charges made against the Port-Royalists are these: that they do not believe in transsubstantiation and in its effect, the real presence of Christ in the Eucharist (this serves as the warrant of a corollary, that they are consciously and deliberately working with the Protestants); and that their strictures on frequent communion, in cases where it is not followed by real penitence and amendment, are contrary to the thought and practice of the church. Pascal names names, cites documents, presents reasons, narrates actions in his emotion-laden defense. At every opportunity he stresses his main point: the Jesuits are making deliberate use of slander, after having defended and excused it as a legitimate tactic, even though they must know that it is contrary to Gospel teaching and that it has been condemned by popes, councils, and saints. Actually they are engaged in something that is self-defeating, for, as he says, "le mal se détruit par sa propre malice."[11] To justify calumny is to destroy one's own believability. But that is not all, for an invisible power works in the situation. Pascal alludes to the miracle of the Sainte-Epine:

Mais Jésus-Christ, en qui elles [les religieuses de Port-Royal] sont cachées pour ne paraître qu'un jour avec lui, vous écoute, et répond pour elles. On l'entend aujourd'hui, cette voix sainte et terrible, qui étonne la nature et qui console l'Eglise. (452)[12]

Pascal reminds his opponents that God will not be mocked; that he has commanded us in the Gospel not to condemn our neighbor without being certain that he is guilty. Exclusion from his kingdom looms for those who make false accusations and their supporters.

An interesting feature of this letter is Pascal's denial at one point of being, as he says, "de Port-Royal." Of course he was so, in a loose sense, but not in the precise sense of being one of the *solitaires*. He had not signed his resources over to the convent in return for a pension, as they had, nor had he taken up residence there. Admitting that he knows and admires the piety and virtue of the Port-Royalists, he insists nonetheless on his independence, and on his status as a third party who has taken up the cause of wronged people and of true doctrine.

The vocabulary of this public defender is full of biblical ideas and imagery; his thought modulates easily into the vein of the Psalmist:

je me suis obligé, moi qui n'ai point de part à cette injure, de vous en faire rougir à la face de toute l'Eglise, pour vous procurer cette confusion salutaire dont parle l'Ecriture, qui est presque l'unique remède d'un endurcissement tel que le vôtre: Imple facies eorum ignominia, et quaerent nomen tuum, Domine. (447)[13]

This one of the most significant moments in the evolution of Pascal's posture in the *Provinciales*. He is now light years away from the ironic, almost nonchalant observer of the first letters; he is no longer attempting to engage in a dialogue (it degenerated into controversy at every turn); he is rather someone who speaks in a prophetic vein, who confronts hardened enemies of God, not hoping to convince them by his arguments but to expose them, to shame them, and to prepare them for a conversion.

Heresy Disproved (Letters 17–18)

Letter 17 (23 January 1657). With this letter the main theme shifts from the examination of Jesuit motives back to questions of doctrine. The matter to be resolved is whether or not heresy has lately arisen in the church. Pascal says that it has not. Certainly he (the writer of the letters) has not been proved heretical; he affirms that there is nothing in his belief or conduct to support such a judgment. Nor can he be included in any accusation of Port-Royal: here he reiterates that he is "not of Port-Royal." But the charge that Jansenius and his followers are heretics requires a more elaborate reply.

First, in a passage that reminds us of the first letters, where ambiguities in the use of the word "grace" had to be made explicit, Pascal points out that "heresy" has had a succession of meanings in the controversy:

Mais vous avez seulement changé leur hérésie selon le temps. Car, à mesure qu'ils se justifiaient de l'une, vos Pères en substituaient une autre, afin qu'ils n'en fussent jamais exempts. Ainsi, en 1653, leur hérésie était sur la qualité des propositions. Ensuite elle fut sur le *mot à mot.* Depuis vous la mîtes dans le coeur. Mais aujourd'hui on ne parle plus de tout cela; et l'on veut qu'ils soient hérétiques s'ils ne signent que le sens de la doctrine de Jansénius se trouve dans le sens de ces cinq propositions. (456) [14]

Untying the knot of the argument in this affair was not in the seventeenth century, nor is it now, an easy task. There is always the risk of omitting something important or of not quite grasping something else or both. For the Jesuits there is a single issue. Jansenius said heretical things that are summed up in the five propositions condemned by the pope; the Port-Royalists and the author of the letters follow Jansenius; therefore, they are heretical.

Pascal meets the challenge head-on, but for him there is a double issue. He states it as a distinction between a matter of faith and a matter of fact. Two things must be settled: (1) are the propositions heretical? and (2) are they, in fact, found in the works of Jansenius? The answer to the first is *yes,* but to the second, a definite *no.* Hence there is no heresy, for no one is contradicting the doctrine of efficacious grace as originally laid down in the Bible and then transmitted and developed within the church by saints, popes, and councils. As for the second question, the answer must be negative, because no one has ever shown by evidence of the proper kind (matters of fact are settled by appeal to evidence of the senses and by reasoning from such evidence) that the condemned statements are present in the pages of Jansenius. Consequently, no one is obliged to assent to the thesis that they are so present. The Jesuits are simply confusing two separate problems; they are insisting abusively on papal infallibility in matters of fact as well as in matters of faith.

Looking, as often, for the reason or cause that explains an effect, he goes behind the statements, ambiguities, and evasions of the Jesuits to their motive. As before, he finds it in their concern for the glory of their society, but the reasoning takes a particular line here because it touches on the prestige of Molina and of his theology, in which the notion of *grâce suffisante* (with its positive implications for the state of human nature and will) is decisive, to the detriment, as the Jansenists see it, of the traditional *grâce efficace* (with its restrictive implications regarding human nature and will). Pascal assumes that the Jesuits are proceeding in two stages: now they attack efficacious grace in the writings of Jansenius, that is, indirectly; later they will feel free to attack it openly and directly.

Pascal writes in letter 17 not to the fathers in general but to one in particular, Père Annat, who had been actively engaged in the anti-Jansenist campaign and who as Louis XIV's confessor was an eminent force in it. This letter, which appears at first to be ironic in intention, returns at the end to the tone of polemic. Although Pascal does not use the word "heretic" as he speaks of his opponents, the conclusion is clear: something heretical is being attempted. In a matter of the utmost importance—the personal relations between man and God—the Jesuits intend, Pascal thinks, to substitute an invention of their own for established and tested beliefs.

Letter 18 (24 March 1657). According to the preceding letter the "sense of Jansenius," alleged to be heretical, had never been defined. Letter 18 takes as its point of departure a statement made by Annat containing two important propositions. First, it is not enough, he says, to say that Jansenius holds the doctrine of efficacious grace. Second, that does not suffice because that doctrine may be held in two ways, (1) one that is heretical and in accord with Calvin, and (2) the other that is orthodox and in accord with the councils, the Thomists, and the "Sorbonnistes." Of course Annat identifies the stand of Jansenius with that of Calvin, to the effect that the will, when moved by grace, has no power to resist. The orthodox view, he says, holds that one always has the power to resist and to refuse the influx of grace.

After citing this passage, Pascal writes triumphantly that there is no heresy in the church: all parties to the dispute consider the position of Calvin to be wrong; everyone agrees that divine grace governs the will in such a way that it may be resisted. However, things are not quite so simple as that, and some crucial further explanation is needed. Pascal presents an argument in which he first sets the view of Calvin in opposition to that of Molina and then gathers up into a synthesis the partial truths contained in the other two. Calvin asserts the inability of man to resist grace (stressing its victorious power), while Molina asserts on the contrary, man's ability always to resist it (exalting human will and its possibility of making meritorious choices). The true position, according to Pascal, is that of St. Augustine and St. Thomas: it affirms that man has always the power to resist grace, but does not always will to use that power. Under the influence of grace he sees on the one hand his mortality and nothingness, and on the other the greatness and the incorruptible goodness of God; in the light of this intuition worldly objects lose their attractiveness for him, and his will turns infallibly but freely to God. In its proper line of operation the will seeks the good that pleases it most, and in this instance it moves on its own and without fail to the good that contains and supersedes all others.

Pascal resolves here a fundamental conflict by taking two extreme views, summed up into ringingly clear propositions, and drawing them into an equilibrium that states the whole truth. It is interesting to note the emergence of a dialectical line of thought at this decisive point in the letters. It will be recalled that during at least part of the period in which he was composing the *Provinciales* Pascal was building up the dossiers of his general apology for the Christian religion. He casts his arguments in this same logical figure again and again in the *Pensées*, three outstanding examples being the treatments of Nature (starting with the infinitely large and the infinitely small), man (starting with simultaneous greatness and wretchedness), and the Bible (starting with the curiously antithetical relationship of the two Testaments). And in the *Ecrits sur la grâce* Pascal simply repeats what he does in the *Provinciales*: Calvin, Molina, and St. Augustine and their positions are fitted into exactly the same triadic pattern.

The weighty question of faith is answerable, then, in a way that is consonant with authority and tradition. By stating at last what was

objectionable in Jansenius—the identity of his position with that of
Calvin—Annat has accomplished something prodigious: the defenders
of efficacious grace find themselves justified by the defenders of
Molina. Pascal relishes the paradox; he even sees in it the hand of
God: "tant la conduite de Dieu est admirable pour faire concourir
toutes choses à la gloire de sa vérité."[15]

Only the question of fact remains. Pascal offers his readers a particularly lucid discussion of this subject. He settles the issue in a way
that meets the criteria of verification that apply to the domain of
matters of fact. There are in us three principles of knowledge: sense,
reason, and faith, each having its distinctive object and the power
of attaining the kind of certainty proper to that object. The dispute
reduces to this: whether or not Jansenius affirms five heretical propositions. To decide it we must ultimately appeal, whatever the intermediate steps in the inquiry may be, to the first of those principles,
to an act of seeing or not seeing the statements in his works. And
so Pascal calls again, as Arnauld had done as early as 1649, for a
formal conference in which the works would be examined. Until that
has been done, Annat has no right to refer to his adversaries as ob-
stinate (in their alleged errors): "car ils sont sans erreurs sur les points
de foi; catholiques sur le droit, raisonnables sur le fait, et innocents
en l'un et en l'autre" (467).[16]

My remarks may give the impression that this letter moves more
or less exclusively on an abstract and doctrinal plane. Actually it is
another production in Pascal's vehement and accusatory style. He
sees himself as seeking peace, but he continues to seek it by means
that will humiliate his opponents. In this letter he renews the familiar
charges of political maneuver and of statements slanderous by design. We sense that the controversy has reached a point at which it
might and should end. After all, from Pascal's point of view, an un-
beatable case has been made against the Jesuits, first indirectly and
ironically, then more and more directly, until few if any holds were
barred: it is now time for the jury of those who have followed the
argument to render a verdict. And yet the triumphant attitude of the
one who has so diligently defended the innocent is qualified by some
dissatisfaction. Pascal seems to have realized at this point in his
enterprise that he has been fighting alone. Many others among the
targets of the Jesuits' campaign might have spoken out but had not
done so. Their patience, their reticence surprise Pascal: "Je les vois
néanmoins si religieux à se taire que je crains qu'il n'y ait en cela

de l'excès."[17] Although theirs is an attitude that he cannot adopt, perhaps he envies them a little as he writes to Annat, "Laissez l'Eglise en paix, je vous y laisserai de bon coeur."[18] Nevertheless, the last note he strikes is that of a fair warning: if the peace that he believes now to have been achieved in the church is disturbed once more, his adversaries should not doubt that some "children of peace" would present themselves, ready to do all in their power to preserve tranquillity.

Pascal made some notes for a nineteenth letter, but it was never finished. The battle was continued in another form and on a more limited subject—the old question of the Jesuit moral system, in the collective work known as the "Ecrits des curés de Paris."[19] Until July of 1658 Pascal was a valued collaborator in this undertaking, and even the probable author of the first, second, fifth, and sixth *écrits*.

Doctrine and Politics

As we have seen in passing, the series as a whole evolves in a definite progression from one rhetorical situation to another. A further point—concerning Pascal's intended readers—deserves mention. He always has in mind an audience of fair-minded people who need and want to be informed of innovations in theology, conduct, and devotion that he takes to be quite mistaken. But he always approaches that audience indirectly: first he writes to a friend (letters 1–10) as an observer of third parties and their behavior; then he composes a set of letters (letters 11–16) that are addressed directly to his Jesuit opponents; and finally (in letters 17–18) he enters into a face to face encounter with one of the leaders of the Society. He offers his summary of the new and—as he believes—unacceptable doctrines and he makes his revelations of Jesuit maneuverings for influence always without turning directly to his audience. As a result the reader is a spectator situated in a zone outside the heat of the rhetoric; he is in a very favorable position to judge the issues fairly. But one might argue that this absence of direct appeals makes him all the more vulnerable to the art and intensity of Pascal.

In any case, whatever his stance, whether he is presenting in his letters little dialogues on points of doctrine, defending his letters as to their style and content, or at the last, trying to reconcile differences and to bring the dispute to a close, Pascal is always working on a single thesis, always answering an attack on the traditional concep-

tion of grace. Since the attackers are substituting a new conception
for the old, he is drawn into an effort to clarify the situation as to
terminology. He senses that he must bring under control the ambiguities of the language in which the exchanges are conducted.

No discussion of these points can be easy, and whoever ventures
to sum up the issue will surely disoblige someone. But the attempt
must be made. What is at stake is two ways of stating the relation
between God and man, and more specifically, between two free beings,
one of whom is uncreated and sovereign while the other is created and
dependent. The question for everyone on both sides of the issue is,
how can these two beings cooperate, how can they act together so
that the free initiative of neither is denied?

Each side has its basic inclination and its respected theoretician.
The Port-Royalists have Jansenius (and, as they think, St. Augustine
behind him); they tend to stress the majesty and justice of God as
opposed to the shortcomings and weaknesses of man and human will.
The Jesuits have as their champion Molina, the sixteenth-century
Spanish theologian; their inclination is to look for positive qualities
in man's nature, to exalt his will power (without denying the importance of God's role in moral life).

The differences come to a focus on this point: whether or not man
is free to refuse the motions of divine grace. As Pascal poses the problem in the eighteenth letter, there are two errors to be avoided: that
of Molina, who thinks that man can refuse grace, and that of Calvin,
who thinks that man cannot refuse grace and that such a motion on
the part of God cannot be frustrated by human will. But this is a
case in which we must find a way to assert simultaneously both propositions, for the error in each instance consists precisely in affirming
only one of the two without regard for the other. Jansenius and St.
Augustine—who have the truth in the matter, according to Pascal—
say that man both has and does not have the power to shut himself
off from grace.

What does this mean? Here, in Pascal's view, the correct procedure
lies in stating that the power to refuse is always there, but it is not
always exercised. There comes a moment in one's spiritual life when
an inspired change occurs in our hearts: we see God, ourselves, and
worldly goods in a true light; we see his greatness, his immutability,
his goodness on the one hand, and, on the other, the illusory value
of worldly things; and in this experience our will chooses God—freely
and infallibly, *but not necessarily*. At this time and in these condi-

tions we *could* refuse his grace, but we never do, because the will naturally directs itself to the greatest good.

This way of understanding and solving the problem is inextricably connected with the experience of a conversion, of a moral about-face, of a new and total commitment. There is only one kind of grace here, and the infallibility of the choice shows it to be *efficace.* The Jesuits posit not one but two kinds of grace: there is *grâce suffisante* as well as *grâce efficace.* And the upshot is that conversion does not operate as before. God provides sufficient grace for all men; it is a kind of spiritual capital that one causes—freely—to fructify on the way to receiving the efficacious grace of salvation. Jansenist-Augustinian grace makes one into a new creature, and that better state has its consequences in one's life; Molinist-Jesuit sufficient grace, given to all at the outset, puts us in a relatively good state from which we may freely work toward one that is better.

The path taken in the face of this alternative has profound implications for the way one conceives of Christian morality and life; and it is not difficult to see how in particular historical circumstances the two positions may gravitate toward rigorism and laxism, respectively. Whatever merits the Molinist position has, whatever backing in theology and precedent, the fact is that Pascal considers it to be a betrayal of an absolutely fundamental tenet of the Christian religion. The doctor to follow on the subject of grace is St. Augustine and not Molina. Pascal takes great pains to straighten out the various senses of grace and heresy that have emerged in the contest; and out of elements that he believes to be orthodox he assembles an impressive ideological structure by which to discern and exhibit the errors of his opponents.

Of course the campaign of the *Provinciales* is not fought simply on the terrain of doctrine: far from it. Pascal is entirely convinced that in the minds of the Jesuits religion and doctrine take a back seat to plans for increasing their power. He sees that design behind the facilities of their morality—and also behind the severity of some of their confessors (the paradox is only apparent: thus they have answers and guidance for all). He sees it behind the resort to slander as a justifiable tactic in defending their cause. Without using the word he often expresses the idea: they are Machiavellian in their willingness to use any means to realize their essentially political ends.

Pascal takes hold of this problem in a characteristic way. The plans, tactics, and devices of the Jesuits present themselves to his mind as

attempts to violate the basic orders of things. They act to overturn
a hierarchy of values and to subvert the higher by the lower. Pascal
is persuaded that in the end the project must fail, because the intangible truth is not subject to alteration by worldly and violent
means. The theme recurs at critical points in Pascal's works; we
shall soon meet it again in the *Pensées*, where it is elaborated in the
great distinction of the three orders—of bodies, minds, and hearts, or
of the worldly, the intellectual, and the spiritual. There he establishes
unbridgeable distances between these domains. He recognizes that
tyrannies and imperialisms try from time to time to subject one order
to another, but he knows that such interferences, based on error or
malice, cannot be lastingly successful.

Chapter Four

The *Pensées*

The Grouping of the Fragments

The most familiar and most constantly influential of Pascal's works is known to us as his *Pensées* or "Thoughts." Pascal did not invent the title; that was done by the editors who prepared the first edition—incomplete and retouched in many places—that appeared posthumously in 1670. The full and more informative title of the volume was *Pensées de M. Pascal sur la religion et sur quelques autres sujets.*[1] The *Pensées* are not a work in the strict sense of something that has been completed. They do not even have the form of a continuous draft. What we have is an ensemble of fragments (about one thousand in all), some as short as a word or two, others running on for a half-dozen or more pages. I say "ensemble," because these are not random thoughts, not discrete, isolated pieces. Pascal set out to write an apology or defense of the Christian religion, and the *Pensées* are a complicated set of notes prepared in connection with the project and determined as to form by his manner of composing.

He seems to have visualized the stages in the process as follows: (1) gathering of materials in the shape of jottings and notes, more or less elaborated; (2) classification of materials, so as to establish the degree of relevance that particular topics and fragments have to the main line of the argument; (3) further development of certain themes present in the classified and retained fragments; and (4) connection and integration of the materials into a finished, discursive whole. Of course Pascal never really reached the last phase; the documents we have belong to steps 1 through 3. There are suggestions as to what was to be done in the last stage, but it is not possible to know what changes Pascal might have made in his outline or what modifications the extant fragments would have undergone in the final work of composition. What we have to read and study is not text but pretext, or even subtext, for some fragments are surely intended only as reminders of topics or assumptions or devices, rather than as elements eventually to appear in the text. In short, the "pensées" or "thoughts" of Pascal consist for the most part of his nonscientific papers as they were found and copied at the time of his death.[2]

Let us now look at the external shape of the *Pensées*. I shall adopt here the convenient presentation of Philippe Sellier, who has used the *Seconde Copie* for his edition. It appears to be closer than the *Première Copie* to the state of the papers at the death of Pascal, and indeed it may have served as the personal reference copy kept by Pascal's sister Gilberte. The texts fall into five sections.

(1) Fragments 1–414 correspond to the outline and classification at which Pascal had arrived in 1658. Here we find twenty-eight titled groups of texts, the assembling and titling having been done by Pascal. This project or outline and its contents serve as an indispensable key to Pascal's thought on religion and "quelques autres sujets."

(2) The second section, made up of seven groups of fragments (415–611), contains the dossiers of texts composed during the preparatory phase of Pascal's undertaking (from the summer of 1656 to May of 1658), materials that he then judged to be irrelevant to his needs or at least less relevant than those selected for the preceding section. Here the most significant passages are no doubt the three groups in which he set down his reflections on miracles. As I mentioned earlier, the miracle of the Sainte-Epine had a profound effect on Pascal as he was in the midst of the campaign of the *Provinciales*. He saw then the usefulness of miracles as confirmations of doctrine. About this nucleus, it seems, his apologetic position grew until he could see that what he wanted was a sequence of arguments that included miracles but did not rely more or less exclusively on them. And so the theme of miracles as proofs occurs prominently in the first section, but Pascal integrates it into a larger plan. This section contains also three groups of miscellaneous thoughts.

(3) The third section (612–79) contains fragments composed in the period 1659–62. It adds six more groups of *pensées* to the series found in the preceding section. It includes also the famous passages on the two mentalities, the *esprit de géométrie* and the *esprit de finesse.*

(4) The fourth section contains a total of seventeen groups of fragments (680–738) that appear to develop or extend fragments and themes broached in the first section. It is probable that Pascal, with his plan in definite form, was proceeding to flesh out essential parts of it. The subjects treated are: the indifference of his reader

to religion and how to overcome it; the corruption of human nature since the Fall; the special status of the Jews; the importance of prophecies as evidence of the truth of the Christian religion.

(5) The final section adds to the foregoing from various sources a number of fragments (seventy-six in all, 739–814), which treat moral and religious subjects but do not appear in the *Copie.* Here are to be found the text of the "Mémorial," the document in which Pascal recorded the conversion experience of the night of 23 November 1654, and also that of the "Mystère de Jesus," an intense meditation on Christ's Passion. Other fragments included here pertain to the Jesuits and the themes of the *Provinciales.*

Three Qualities of the Christian Religion

Attempts to summarize the contents of the project of 1658 are unsatisfactory because of what one necessarily leaves out, and also because it is impossible to summarize without bringing Pascal's thought to a focus that is likely to be too fine, too limiting. The tentative, the allusive, the connotative nature of the *Pensées* rarely comes across as one would like. Any summary is best viewed as an entering wedge for the actual experience of reading the texts. That said, it is not difficult to recover the main ideas and articulations of the argument, for there is always in Pascal a fundamental aspiration to lucidity and coherence.

We may take as a starting point some brief remarks he makes in the early set of fragments arranged under the title "Ordre." The problem he wishes to solve presents itself to him and becomes concrete for him in three steps. (1) The Christian religion is defensible; it lends itself to the composition of an apology. Why? For these reasons: it is *vénérable*, worthy of respect; it is *aimable*, attractive, desirable; and it is *vraie*, true, appealing and satisfying to the mind. The sequence of the adjectives is important, for it reveals the general sequence into which Pascal's thoughts and notes are intended to fit, in spite of the meanders, repetitions, and near-repetitions that result from his way of working. One comes first to respect the Christian religion; then one is drawn by and to it; and finally one comes to see that it is true. (2) Pascal lays down the line of reasoning to be developed under each topic: venerable, because it has understood man and the human condition; lovable because it promises and provides the true good (one might say equally well, the good truth); and true, because of the many proofs that may be found for it. (3) With the foregoing as a background, Pascal turns his reflective and inventive powers to the task of assembling about each of the three leading terms (and their subdivisions) notes that he expects some day to put in order before proceeding to give them their final form and expression.

Why it is Venerable

What are some of the characteristic distinctions and reasons regarding the quality of Christianity as venerable? In what sense has it known man in a peculiarly adequate way? The first proposition to which Pascal addresses himself is this: that our human nature is corrupt—corrupt because its fundamental powers and tendencies are in such a state that they do not function properly; they are doomed to frustration. Take, for example, our cognitive powers: our reason, our senses, our imagination. Unreliable to begin with, they perversely work against each other so as to compound errors. We want to have knowledge that is true and stable; instead our usual state is uncertainty. Or take our feelings and desires (the heart as opposed to mind and reason): here Pascal pictures vividly the diversity, the contradictions, the vanities of human wishes. We want, as our supreme goal, to attain the sovereign good, happiness; but what are we to do in the face of all the definitions that have been given to that term? And how are we to overcome the fault that underlies all others in the sphere of morality: the inconstancy, the essential mobility of our desires? As Pascal puts it in fragment 24, "Condition de l'homme: Inconstance, ennui, inquiétude."[3]

The description that Pascal gives of man's plight—as a being who wants and pursues the true and the good but cannot achieve them—has its analogue in society. We should like to have it that justice would be the basis of the social order. Pascal sees instead irrational custom and its mental counterpart, opinion, as the principles at work in society. They work on the surface, that is, for underneath the crust of custom he discovers force as the basis of law and the state. Continuing the attack, he takes up a very old theme and embroiders new variations on it: he shows us how, as we move from one country to another, from one social order to another, the diversity of habits, values, codes, institutions makes it impossible for us to locate any natural or universal principles of justice: "Vérité au-deçà des Pyrénées, erreur au-delà."[4] The conclusion points to another frustration. Although man wants justice, he cannot attain it; what he has in society is, at its best, a not very admirable order based on self-interest—or, in Pascal's vocabulary, concupiscence.

Such analyses present us with a picture of man in a tragic impasse. In the hope of finding guidance one may consult the philosophers. To Pascal this almost always means moral philosophers, and even more narrowly than that, the Stoics and Epicureans. But they have in fact little light to shed on the problem. What they do is to lead us in more technical language and by their hardening into opposed sects to the same despairing conclusions about man: "Quelle chimère est-ce donc que l'homme? quelle nouveauté, quel monstre, quel chaos, quel sujet de contradictions, quel prodige? Juge de toutes choses, imbécile ver de terre, dépositaire du vrai, cloaque d'incertitude et d'erreur, gloire et rebut de l'univers" (515; fr. 131).[5]

Leaving the terrain that he calls "nature," Pascal makes an important transition to a higher and more inclusive level—that of the church and Christian religion. He asserts that Christian teaching has always emphasized the duplicity and weakness of man, that the portrait he has been composing on the basis of observation and experience corresponds to, and is indeed identical to, one side of the human condition as it appears in a supernatural perspective. From the beginning the Christian religion has understood man ("a bien connu l'homme"); it has known his uncertainties, his variations, his social illusions, and his ultimate vanity. (One might add that the tone and themes of Pascal's reflection are characteristic of one tendency in Christian thought—the Augustinian tradition: that in large part is what the controversy of the Jansenists and the Jesuits is about, for the latter were setting up something like a new ancestry for moral theology.)

Of course the religious perspective makes it possible not only to describe the situation correctly but also to explain it. The frustrating gap in our minds and lives between what is and what ought to be (and, it seems, can never be) is the consequence of original sin. Our intuition of what ought to be is a recollection of Eden, and what is is what we have fallen into through the sin of Adam. Each of us is a "roi dépossédé," a "dispossessed king" (513; fr. 116). Pascal sees and stresses the paradox in this argument, where an enigma is explained by a mystery ("le plus incompréhensible de tous"—"the most incomprehensible of all," 515; fr. 131), but he is convinced that this is the only satisfactory solution.

The reasoning moves next to the notion of "remedy." The problem in Eden and in every age since then has been that man misuses his freedom, turns away from God, puts himself at the center of everything, and lets himself become attached to the world and its goods. The remedy can only consist in a conversion, in a return—insofar as possible—to his former relationship with God.

And so, because of these lights, the Christian religion is *vénérable*.

Why it is Lovable

Pascal expects that his reader, having followed him thus far, will begin to change according to the natural working of desire and will. The endless pursuit of relative goods and truths is seen to be empty, vain: let it be relinquished then in favor of a search for God. He is the Truth and the aim of all our knowing powers; he is the Good and the joy of all desires. Although this God is infinite and transcendent, he is accessible to all through Jesus Christ, the mediator. Through him there is for us the prospect of possessing God inchoately and partially in this life, which is conceived by Pascal as a time of trial on the way to beatitude. Such a remedy is *aimable*, so much so that it would seem impossible for us not to choose it. However, a truly effective and unswerving love for it is not ultimately in our power. For that kind of love we must have faith, and we cannot give ourselves faith: that comes strictly from God; it is a "don de Dieu." In fact, quite apart from the question of salvation, we cannot by the natural operation of our minds even know that God exists; we have no proportion to such a being. "S'il y a un Dieu, il est infiniment incompréhensible, puisque n'ayant ni parties ni bornes, il n'a nul rapport à nous. Nous sommes donc incapables de connaître ni ce qu'il est, ni s'il est" (550; fr. 418).[6] So much for the various demonstrations of God's existence proposed by the philosophers. And *a fortiori* his nature and intentions elude our finite capacities.

If, then, we are now drawn to something that we cannot have except by an intimate gift that depends on the divine will, what to do here and now? Pascal's answer is that one must remove the obstacles—"ôter les obstacles"—and put oneself in a faith-seeking posture. The preparation required is not simple or superficial. It calls for a drastic reorientation of the mind and the will. Once more we return to the two aspects of human nature that are most relevant to moral life: *raison* and *coeur*, reason and heart. The diagnosis that pictured the human condition started from our innate tendencies toward truths and goods; the remedy proposed complete satisfaction of those tendencies; and it is not surprising to see that they are profoundly involved here in the treatment of seekers after faith. Two of the three adjectives that preside over the whole discussion—*aimable* and *vraie*—are pertinent precisely because the qualities they designate appeal to those two parts of the psyche.

Now an absolutely fundamental triad comes into view. The terms in it refer to what Pascal calls the three means of believing, the "trois moyens de croire." They are reason, custom, and inspiration. The first two are the familiar innate tendencies in a new and positive guise; and they are subject to action on the part of the apologist and the reader. The third occurs only on God's initiative.

Pascal must continue to reason with reason for the sake of faith. Although to demonstrate the existence and the attributes of God is not possible, by borrowing devices from his calculus of probabilities Pascal can—or asserts that he can—demonstrate that a disposition to believe is not contrary to reason. Here the wager (the "pari") has its place: the famous attempt to show that betting on the existence of God is advisable and even compelling, given the high stakes and the favorable odds. In the passage Pascal first points out to his imagined interlocutor that he cannot avoid a wager—in fact he is already wagering ("vous êtes embarqué," "you are embarked" and engaged in the game just by being alive and by living in a certain way), then develops the terms of the argument in detail. He adapts his method of calculating probabilities in gambling to the situation at hand. There are three things to consider: what is to be risked, what may be won, and what the odds are. Each of us has one life to wager, infinite or eternal life to gain, and the odds are even. These essentially quantitative factors are assembled into a complex *a fortiori* argument reducible finally to something like this: if you are willing to do something in relatively unpromising circumstances, you will surely be willing to do it in circumstances that are quite attractive. More specifically: (1) even if there were only a finite amount of life to be gained, one would be inclined to bet, but since the possible gain is infinite, one would surely be willing to do so; and (2) even if the odds were unfavorable—to the extent of offering one chance of winning against an infinite number of chances of losing—one would still be inclined to bet, but the odds are in fact even—one chance of winning and one chance of losing—and so one would be all the more willing to do so. Pascal concludes triumphantly: "Et ainsi notre proposition est dans une force infinie quand il y a le fini à hasarder, à un jeu où il y a pareils hasards de gain que de perte, et l'infini à gagner."[7] There is, therefore, no "reason" for the reason to put obstacles in the way as one moves toward assent.

Then only the heart, the seat of desires and passions, remains as a source of difficulties. The way to proceed is not by reasoning but through habituation. By behaving as if one believes, by repeated acts of devotion, by living according to Christian precepts one acquires in time a new disposition toward the world and its distractions. As the scenario unfolds, Pascal's reader commits himself intellectually and morally to a state of readiness for faith and to a search for the means of finding and fixing that readiness. Naturally he wishes to know whether what attracts him is true or not, and that brings him to the third pole about which Pascal's reflection gravitates, the proofs and marks of truth that may be presented for the Christian religion.

Why it is True

In the apologetic argument there are two propositions to be proved: (1) that human nature is corrupt; and (2) that there is a Redeemer. The first is taken care of by the treatment of the Christian religion as *vénérable*. The proofs consist in pointing out, on the basis of common experience ("par la nature" in Pascal's phrase), the contradictions and other puzzling aspects of human nature and destiny.

To prove the second proposition requires a more technical effort, an effort of biblical exegesis; and when Pascal speaks of "preuves" in the *Pensées*, he is usually referring to that effort. In fragment 482 he lists twelve items under the heading of "preuves":

PREUVES.—1° La religion chrétienne, par son établissement, par elle-même établie si fortement, si doucement, étant si contraire à la nature.—2° La sainteté, la hauteur et l'humilité d'une âme chrétienne.—3° Les merveilles de l'Ecriture sainte.—4° Jésus-Christ en particulier.—5° Les apôtres en particulier.—6° Moïse et les prophètes en particulier.—7° Le peuple juif.—8° Les prophéties.—9° La perpétuité: nulle religion n'a la perpétuité.—10° La doctrine, qui rend raison de tout.—11° La sainteté de cette loi.—12° Par la conduite du monde. (562)[8]

And what will the effect of these proofs be? Pascal answers the ques-

tion in a concluding sentence that summarizes the intention and value
of his whole undertaking.

Il est indubitable qu'après cela on ne doit pas refuser, en considérant
ce que c'est que la vie, et que cette religion, de suivre l'inclination de la
suivre, si elle nous vient dans le coeur; et il est certain qu'il n'y a nul
lieu de se moquer de ceux qui la suivent. (562) [9]

He wants to arouse, encourage, and justify an attitude that disposes
one not to refuse the inclination (that is, the inspiration) to follow
the Christian religion, if that inclination appears.

But, to return to the list of "preuves": it is not so much a list of
proofs as of topics, of places where proofs may be found. Fragment
402 gives us an idea of how the topics might be worked out.

> Preuves de la religion.
> Morale. / Doctrine. / Miracles. / Prophéties.
> Figures. (549; fr. 402) [10]

What he expects to do in this phase of his project—the proving phase—
is to show us, in connection with any particular point of understanding or belief and its claim to be true, that that item is justifiable as an
example of elevated morality, an explanatory doctrine, a miraculous
intervention or confirmation, the realization of a prophecy, the clari-
fication of a passage in Scripture that must not be taken exclusively
in a literal sense.

As helpful as they are, these lists do not do justice to the texts.
Pascal's mind—fertile, perceptive, ingenious, confident—sees an indefinite number of inferences. Taken together they constitute a proof by
convergence rather than by demonstration (by which I mean a single
discursive sequence with a Q.E.D. at the end). Sometimes he assembles a quasi-mathematical argument, as in the fragment on the *pari*
(not based, strictly speaking, on Scripture, but it has indispensable
scriptural elements). Sometimes he adopts the syllogistic mode, as
when he uses his list of "marks of truth" in order to argue that they
are found in the Christian but not in the other religions. For proving
the truth of Christian beliefs makes it possible to disprove those of
others: Egyptians, Romans, Mohammedans, Chinese. Or again he reasons dialectically, as when he takes the two opposed parts of the Bible
(the two Testaments) and adjusts them to each other with Jesus

Christ as the unifying principle. Or, in still another vein, he may argue from facts, pragmatically, to show that the working of miracles and accomplishment of prophecies are visible signs that divine power is being exercised in the world.

In the diversity that may be detected in every one of these lines of proof, there is something common to all: a concern to relate them to the exigencies of human nature. Pascal knows that the mind expects reasons, and he provides reasons in abundance. He knows that some of the strongest "proofs" come from habit, from the operations of the "machine," a term that applies not only to the body, but also to the heart, and occasionally to the whole of human nature, insofar as it is subject to fixation by repeated acts. Pascal accords an important place to such behavior.

This complex ensemble of proving activities serves to bring our contending ideas and impulses into a provisional harmony, to move us toward certainty, and to keep us in a stable orientation toward God. But their effect falls short of conviction: that comes from inspiration, which lies beyond proof. It is not a consequent that depends logically on some antecedent; it is an intuitive experience that has the immediacy of a sensation and the self-evident quality of a principle. In that experience (as Pascal knew from firsthand) one comes to a certainty that guarantees everything else—all that the would-be believer has been thinking, saying, and doing as a seeker.

Meanings and Orders

The preceding résumé, which is only one of several possible ways of assembling into a rough sequence the main arguments of the apology, introduces us to Pascal's choice of topics and of psychological and moral vocabulary. We can already perceive something of his originality as he takes his place in the Augustinian tradition of Christianity with its emphasis on the consequences of original sin, the experience of conversion, the concept of God as transcendent judge, and man's urgent need for grace. But we can come closer to understanding his personal mark, his creative impulse if, in addition to pulling the fragments into a single line, we study the design and movement immanent in the fragments themselves. This way of looking at them has the advantage of bringing us into the middle of Pascal's distinctive habit of thought and language. It conforms more closely to the actual state of the *Pensées*: they are elements in a composition that was frozen at a certain moment in the process of invention, rather like a marble block abandoned by the sculptor after a figure and a face had begun to emerge.

In the first place we cannot make sense out of Pascal's words unless we know how he assigns meanings to them. The answer to this question opens up one of the most peculiar features of the *Pensées*. Like Descartes, Pascal knew, admired, and used the method of geometry. In the fragmentary document usually known by the title "De l'esprit géométrique" he once summarized the ideal of that method: "tout définir, tout prouver"—to define everything (apart from a few terms whose meanings are intuitively known) and to prove everything. By the first of these phrases he meant to define everything univocally, to fix once and for all a single meaning for every term, so that whenever it occurred thereafter one could substitute the definition for it. Term and definition would be interchangeable in discourse that would be perfectly lucid. But one of the most notable things about the *Pensées* is that the meanings and values of words shift constantly. According to their intellectual bent, readers are either fascinated or irritated by this procedure. Be that as it may, Pascal was convinced (if one judges from his practice) that univocal language would not serve his apologetic purpose.

Many instances could be cited of this dynamic and nongeometrical way of defining words. One may safely say, I think, that every important term in the *Pensées* is involved in some kind of semantic paradox. Take, for example, the famous sentence, "Le coeur a ses raisons que la raison ne connaît point."[11] It is true for Pascal—and we would doubtless be willing to agree—that the "heart" is the seat of feeling and love or desire; he takes it here, however, as a faculty of knowing; it provides not only the first principles on which reason builds but also certain insights not accessible to reason at all. Or take "reason" itself: Pascal takes pleasure in calling it corrupt, and yet the *Pensées* assume and often use explicitly a positive concept of reason; it has a role to play at every stage of the argument; we can see its duplicity and the likelihood of sudden reversals of meaning in the formula, "Soumission et usage de la raison, en quoi consiste le vrai christianisme."[12] Or again, "imagination": Pascal decries it in fragment 44 (504) as "cette maîtresse d'erreur et de fausseté"—"that mistress of error and falsehood"—and yet the extraordinary power of the great fragment (199) on the disproportion of man depends in large part on the fact that the visible stellar universe is as nothing beside the invisible, but imaginable stars and spaces lying beyond it; that is the *infini en grandeur*, and it has its exact pendant as we go in the opposite direction: the smallest things we can see grow bigger and bigger as imagination evokes for us smaller and smaller bodies or particles, and worlds within worlds, each complete with a full range of creatures. Or take "man": what a package of shifting and contradictory qualities he is! In the fragment just mentioned he is nothing, a *néant* when set against the stars; but compared with the infinitely small, he is a colossus; in other fragments he is a thinking reed, a *roseau pensant*, the weakest in nature, for his life can be so easily snuffed out, and yet he is a prodigious thing in creation, since he knows the universe and what is happening to him: of that the universe knows nothing. Or, once more, take "custom": it is clearly something to be distrusted, because it blinds us and reinforces our prejudices; on the other hand, as a second nature it is a source of certainty without which a conversion of the kind Pascal proposes could not occur. Or again, the Bible: from it arises two accounts of what God has done in response to man's need and hope for redemption—did the Messiah come or did he not?—and, furthermore, our response to that question requires us to face the fact that critical parts of the Old Testament differ in mode of statement (they must be interpreted figuratively) from the New Testament (where the language is literal). Or again, take "goodness" and "truth": Pascal uses *bien* and *vérité* of realities that are present and active in everyone's life, but in the context of eternity and divinity, our happiness and truth are poor, indeed, and he may say here as elsewhere, "le fini s'anéantit en la présence de l'infini."[13] And finally there is the notion of "infinity," without which Pascal as a scientist and as an apologist would have very little to say: he sees a quantitative infinite in number, space, time, and movement, but he understands it contrastively—in the light of a divine infinite, in whom the *infini en grandeur* and the *infini en petitesse* unite, and whose divine person is both hidden and not hidden to man.

One could go on almost indefinitely in this way. The pages of the *Pensées* are dotted with these and other antitheses and paradoxes that testify to a mobile, analogical technique of defining and using words. It disconcerts most readers, and that is, no doubt, the effect that Pascal (the "Christian Socrates" as some called him) intends. If words and things exist and behave in this curious manner, our faculties are left in a state of shock.

Matters begin to come clear if—leaving Pascal's definitions and looking now at his mode of reasoning—we recognize this semantic confusion or variation for what it is: an element in a dialectical process. The process has two phases, positive and negative. In the former Pascal develops oppositions with the skill of a virtuoso; in the latter he finds some way of reconciling them, usually by locating some third term to which they may be adjusted. One of his favorite themes is the simultaneous greatness and misery of man; and he amplifies it to the point of finally exclaiming: "quel chaos, quel monstre!" But this is the negative side of the argument, intended to make us as aware as we can be of the co-presence of opposite qualities in a given subject. The positive part of the cycle begins when we perceive that the "greatness" of man is really the result of pride, which can become humility (without loss of dignity) as man sees himself in relation to God; and his wretchedness, traceable to concupiscence and its appetites, can become penitence, once man turns to God and lets him redress the inclination to evil. The unbearable paradox of human nature, the tension between the two postulations, as Baudelaire called them later, is modified and harmonized by the effective presence of God.

We may note another instance of such reconciliation in Pascal's reading of the Bible. That book is the locus of an extremely significant paradox, and not to resolve it would be catastrophic. On the one hand, the Old Testament account of God's ways with men and of the promise, apparently unfulfilled, of a Messiah; on the other hand, the New Testament account of that Messiah's life, his teaching, and its lasting effects: if that contradiction cannot be removed, the continuity and perpetuity of the Christian religion evaporate. Pascal clears up the difficulty by an exegetical strategem (not original with him, of course): by interpreting crucial passages in the Old Testament as figures or allegories, he can go on to treat the Gospels as accounts of prophecies that have been fulfilled and show that Christ is, in fact, the hero of the Old Testament as well as the New.

And so the habit of defining words (and things) in terms of opposites—which must be accepted at least temporarily, if one is to make sense of the *Pensées*—is nicely fitted to the dialectic of Pascal. In fact, neither can be understood without the other. The dialectic is based on the formulas known to all who have opened the *Pensées*: "l'homme sans Dieu" and "l'homme avec Dieu," with the negative phase of the argument corresponding to the former, man without God, and the positive phase to the latter, man with God.

This essentially simple set of procedures gives a rich and complex result for several reasons. I shall mention two here and reserve a third for later discussion. (1) Any fragment may be conceived and written by Pascal in a perspective that is primarily negative or positive; or it may, as in a microcosm, summarize his total vision. There are innumerable degrees on the scale between the poles and varying degrees, as well, of approximation to the point where corruption and redemption—the two master themes—come into balance. (2) Pascal has recourse to a hierarchical arrangement for another and very important way of posing the problems he wishes to treat. I am referring to the famous fragment 308 on the "trois ordres," the three orders of bodies, minds, and charity; it begins: "La distance infinie des corps aux esprits figure la distance infiniment plus infinie des esprits à la charité, car elle est surnaturelle."[14]

The senses of many fundamental terms have then to be reinterpreted on three instead of two levels. Pascal goes to great pains to establish in our minds his conviction that the three orders or terrains are infinitely distant from each other. And yet—the same word "order" applies to these distinct planes of reality, so its meaning must be taken as analogical. Pascal speaks of the *grandeurs* proper to each order: each has its kingdoms, its victories, its brilliance, its representatives. There are kings, captains, and plutocrats on the level of bodies—they live in the flesh; there are the *gens d'esprit*, the great geniuses on the level of mind and intellectual accomplishment; at the top there are the saints. Pascal even mentions two models for the upper levels: Archimedes and Christ, respectively.

When our language signifies in relation to the hierarchical scheme, we have something rather different from the two-step procedure, where words have values and connotations according to the two regimes under which they appear, man-without-God and man-with-God. But it is not hard to translate from the double to the triple ordering, from the diptych to the triptych. The situation of man-apart-from-God corresponds to the first and second levels of the hierarchical scale—that is, to men and things as bodies first, then to men as thinking beings; man-with-God corresponds to the top level of charity and supernature. The distinction of orders adds metaphysical and moral depth to the discussion—metaphysical, because it makes explicit three instead of two kinds of being; moral, because on the affective side of human nature it places at infinite removes from each other acts of concupiscence and acts of charity.

The Analysis of Assent

The way of thinking that I have been describing can be carried out in a soliloquy. That means, however, that we have seen only one side of the situation or matrix that underlies the *Pensées* insofar as they are determined by an apologetic project. Pascal assumes that he has the truth, but that is only half the picture: the ultimate center of attention is his reader or interlocutor. What he knows he must communicate to another person, who may be indifferent or hostile. Here we pass from the dialectical or logical aspect of the *Pensées* to their rhetorical aspect. Pascal's analysis of the problem of assent— the faculties concerned, the changes through which their operations pass—is elliptical; nowhere does he treat it extensively. What we need is a fragment where Pascal is led to exemplify the whole process.

A good place to look is in the *pari*. A caveat, though, to begin with: the act of wagering is only one step among several that are shown in fragment 418. It is not the goal of everything else; it is emphatically not the last word in spirituality. Pascal is partly to blame for the error we may fall into. It takes such an effort to grasp the details in the middle of the fragment that we may miss some important statements made at the beginning and at the end. The wager on the existence of God is only one moment in a long process of spiritual ascent. (If Pascal's language had been English, he might have been intrigued by the possible play on the words "ascent" and "assent.")

For us the interesting thing is that in a relatively short space— three or four pages—Pascal writes a kind of dialogue, in the course of which the interlocutor passes from (1) admitting the inability of reason to demonstrate the existence of God to (2) accepting the thesis, which is justified by mathematical reasoning, that it is preferable to bet on God's existence rather than not to do so to (3) embarking on a way of living that will moderate his passions. This faith-seeking way of thinking and behaving will, Pascal suggests, lead to (4) certification by grace and faith. In traditional rhetoric assent appears to be a rather simple act, but as Pascal conceives it, it becomes quite complex. Part of the difference must be due to the fact that in the usual procedure one uses premises and prejudices accepted by the audience as the starting points of one's presentation; and on that basis one can build with good chances of success. The special problem of the *Pensées* lies in this, that the writer aims to change radically the ideas of the reader—and not simply his ideas: what is desired is also a basic change in moral posture, a conversion.

Using the *pari* as I have proposed, and completing it with data drawn from other passages and fragments, we arrive at a series of states, which are distinguishable but not separable in any mechanical way: (1) the *original disposition* or point of departure: it may vary— with regard to religion—from ignorance to indifference to hostility; (2) the *onset of doubt*, when self-awareness appears and unavoidable questions present themselves; (3) the *search*, a truly critical stage of the whole process, and once Pascal reaches it or causes his reader to reach it, real progress has been made, for the problems of human nature and destiny have emerged into the light. Here one should recall the sentence from Pascal's meditation on the mystery of Jesus: "Tu ne me chercherais pas si tu ne m'avais trouvé."[15] Inspiration is present at the start as well as at the end of the way. The beginning of the search is followed (4) by a *review of proposed solutions*: Pascal and his interlocutor turn to common sense, to philosophers, and to the history of religions. Next comes (5) a *decision*, motivated by reasoning—possibly in several modes—and on that basis one accepts provisionally in an act of discernment and judgment the Christian explanation of the human condition and its corresponding remedy. But this intellectual act is not enough: since Pascal sees the need for an effort in conduct as well as in thought, we must add to the provisional affirmation reached by the mind another stage, (6) a consequent *moral quality or habit*; and now both *raison* and *coeur* are so inclined that the divine gift of faith may occur. We may count in the next place (7) a *state of grace and faith* that results from the mysterious intervention of God. That is accompanied (8) by *certainty*, by the realization that what once has been granted provisionally is indeed true, and by the assurance that the choice of a new way of life is indeed correct.

For Pascal himself the truth tends to take on the status of an intuition; to grasp it he needs little or no development other than, perhaps, the construction of *schémas* or telegraphic formulas. However, this comprehensive insight has to be broken down and fitted to the mechanism of assent in the person addressed. Pascal wants, first, to pacify that person's mind, not by any attempt to dull or circumvent it, but by going along with it as far as possible, by providing at the limits of its reach a kind of *ortho-doxy*—right opinion—and then, in the second place, he wants to point out and recommend the means by which the passions may be quieted. It may be tempting to speak of a "leap of faith" as a requirement imposed on the reader of the *Pensées*, but the expression is not appropriate. Pascal foresees a long process or itinerary; he intends to make the transitions smooth as one moves from stage to stage; he wishes precisely to get away from the sensation of making irrational leaps. He recognizes with utter candor that the initiative leading to faith is not in him and his rhetoric but in God and his love. Apart from that basic restriction reasonings, proofs, arguments abound in the *Pensées*; and the last stage—conviction and conversion—implies a vindication of reason as a propaedeutic faculty and looks forward to further exploration of the content and validity of what one believes.

A comparison with Descartes throws light on the fifth and sixth steps of the sequence: the moments when the decision is made to accept conditionally the thesis that God exists and then to act accordingly. There is a point in the *Discours de la méthode* at which, after formulating the principal rules of his intellectual method, Descartes realizes that he needs a provisional morality. The idea is that no truth of morality appears to be certain (all he is sure of at that stage is the procedure he will follow in his various inquiries), and that, nonetheless, he must have some maxims to live by. And so he assumes four principles: (1) he will obey the laws and follow the customs of his native country; (2) he will be firm and resolute in his actions, once he has decided on a line of conduct; (3) he will try to conquer himself rather than to outdo fortune, to change his desires rather than the world; and (4) he will review the various occupations of men, in order to make the best possible choice for himself. Descartes expects that later in his investigations he will arrive at a definitive morality, which will be substituted for the temporary one— or if the result is merely to confirm what he assumed at the outset, at least his principles will have been certified by reason.

The contrast with Pascal's *as if* is instructive. His wagerer starts out on his spiritual journey with an opinion and a kind of life that is entailed by it; and he, too, looks forward to the time when his provisional code will be ratified. But that result will not come from any act or acts of reason; he will know by faith that his wager was proper and right, that the diversions and baneful pleasures of his former life cannot be compared with his life and prospects as a Christian. The rationalism of Descartes, which is pure in its kind, is less complicated than the equally pure position taken by Pascal, which requires him to make the utmost use of reason in all the preparatory steps, and then to make way for suprarational light (actually seen in the heart: "Dieu sensible au coeur; c'est le coeur qui sent Dieu et non la raison"),[16] and finally to use reason within the perspective set by his faith.

The "Ordre du Coeur"

In discussing certain traits of method in the *Pensées* I have concentrated on Pascal's dialectical way of thinking about his beliefs and on the evolution through which his reader must pass if he is some day to share those beliefs. One of these elements is doctrinal, and may be summed up in the contrast of man-without-God and man-with-God (an antithesis that may be elaborated into the distinction of the three orders) and the other psychological, which includes an analysis of assent. When these two active ingredients are brought together and adjusted to each other, the combination results in the reflections set down in the fragments of the *Pensées*. Pascal relates the truth that he sees to the mental and moral states of someone else; and those states, moods, attitudes are places of invention and starting points for the working of Pascal's creative powers. Ideas arise at any one of those points (which correspond roughly to the chapter headings of the *projet*); they are combined into phrases or statements; and statements may grow into arguments and even longer textual units. But whatever the theme that is being developed, whatever the specification of Christian truth that is occurring, the object of belief and assent is always one and the same: God. This kind of composition exemplifies what Pascal calls the "order of charity" or the "order of the heart."

Jésus-Christ, saint Paul ont l'ordre de la charité, non de l'esprit, car ils voulaient échauffer, non instruire. Saint Augustin de même. Cet ordre consiste principalement à la digression sur chaque point qui a rapport à la fin, pour la montrer toujours. (539; fr. 298, reading "échauffer" instead of "rabaisser")[17]

Digression is, then, the proper way of dealing with the reader; indeed, it has the most authoritative precedents that one can cite where moving and disposing the heart are concerned. And now another source of complexity in Pascal's thought and expression becomes apparent. His dialectic of man and God is remarkable for its clarity, for its regular progression from contradictions to unifications. The pattern is repeated so often that he seems occasionally to be fitting terms into something like algebraic formulas. His rhetoric must take account not only of ideas (which are relatively easy to control and arrange) but also of psychological states and tendencies (which are much harder to manage, though they may be assembled into a sequence from indifference or hostility to conviction). To the linear modes of exposition implied in reasoning about belief and in adapting to inner changes expected in the reader, Pascal adds a complication, the digressive order of the heart.

One can see the advantages it has. It does not ask of the reader the effort of attention that would be needed for an exclusively sequential treatment, and it offers him immediate satisfactions. Pascal is free to start with any of the topics that are relevant to the line of assent—such as "vanity," "wretchedness," "falsity of other religions"— and discuss it digressively; and yet no matter what direction is taken, the end is always in sight. Although he certainly does not neglect the overall shape of the argument or the matching line of an evolving attitude toward religion, Pascal never calls upon his reader to wait for the end of the dialectic or of the discourse to be enlightened or moved. He manages to bring into a single focus the force of argument, the stages of psychological change, and the satisfaction of immediate insight.

The *Pensées*: Conclusion

Here we have studied for the most part one dimension of this extraordinary work—the ideas in it and the way in which they are related to each other and to an ever-present though often only implied listener or reader. To be more complete we should have to study not only Pascal's way of making words signify and move in shared discourse, but also the imagery he uses, now to suggest ideas, at other times to reinforce them; we should have to follow the changing pathos, the emotions that underlie and echo the ideas and images. Here are a few samples. Pascal imagines man facing nature that, in one direction, stretches without end into space, and in the other, disappears into unimaginable smallness; or shut up with his fellow-men in a dungeon, as he waits for the order of execution to arrive; or afloat on a "milieu vaste" that is never still; or as a thinking reed, claiming his dignity as one who knows against all the unknowing size and power of the universe; or, in the most fundamental image of all, man as the *chercheur*, the seeker, turning back from diversions to his origin and end. Pascal feels deeply, and he communicates those feelings to us: his indignation at the thought of indifferent men who never bother to ask or face the important questions; his joy and fear as he evokes his God; his astonishment at the contradictions of human nature and action; his triumphant excitement as he races through the demonstration of the wager; his marveling at the supernatural sequences that he reads in the Bible; his unfailing assurance as he goes about the exacting and delicate task he has set for himself.

From these fragments we shall never have a work that is entire; we must be satisfied with a design partly carried out. We shall never be able to fit the fragments into a smooth sequence, though that idea has tempted numerous editors. The *Pensées* and, more particularly, the apologetic texts found in them are not like the parts of a jigsaw puzzle where a finished picture has been cut arbitrarily into pieces that may with patience be reassembled. They are more like the *tesserae* of a mosaic, each of which maintains its identity, its contours, its rough edges at the same time that it enters into an ensemble. But even here the comparison often fails, for the texts seem to assert themselves like monads whose nature is to reflect the whole of which they are parts. Let me try a military figure: we have no doubt of what Pascal's objective was; we can recover almost to the point of certainty what the strategy would have been; many of the tactics have been devised, others are being worked out. And yet, we still cannot see how everything would have been determined and coordinated, nor can we know what revisions Pascal would have made. Even the overall plan might not have remained untouched: Pascal said himself that in composing a work the last thing one discovers is what to put first.

Of one thing we can be sure. Pascal would not have published his papers in the form in which we have them. In my opinion it is incorrect to argue, as some have done, that Pascal's "world view" is such that only fragments can do justice to it and that it could not eventuate in any other shape.[18] All the indications are that what he intended and thought possible was something like the *Provinciales*, a genre in which he knew he excelled. If I may venture one last comparison, I think that a time would have arrived when he would have said, as Poussin once did on completing a picture, "Je n'ai rien négligé.[19] Poussin meant, it would seem, that the picture had been fully thought out and worked out, that it was free of rough transitions or visible brushmarks—a pure image. What Pascal left us is not such a picture but a book of sketches that have all the fascination and ambiguity of the unfinished. Some of them refer to the overall design, which is rendered from different viewpoints and with changing perspectives; most of them refer to details or particular areas, and here there is a great deal of overlapping, of variation in development and finish; but everywhere we feel the presence of a sovereign impulse that returns time after time—over a period of years—to the same basic schema and moves it toward realization. Some sketches, set aside, suggest other concerns and hint at other compositions.

The tentative discursive order of the *Pensées*, though real and important, counts perhaps for less than the kind of immediate unity that shines through their multiplicity. Part of the secret derives from Pascal's fine insight into the nature of assent and another part of it from the purity of his dialectic. But there is more. He once wrote, "Il faut avoir une idée de derrière et juger de tout par là" ("You must have an idea in the back of your mind and judge everything by that"). In this little sentence he defined the way of thinking that he took to be most valid in the matters that interest men most. We must try to recover that idea, give it what life we can, and bring it to bear on our reading of the fragments. Then they have a chance to say what they mean and to evoke each other in an authentic way. I think the idea in question can only be the infinite person who emerges from the Bible. Because he is the subsistent truth and the subsistent good, he is the criterion by which everything else must—at least eventually—be judged. This idea of an infinite who abounds in consequences for everything finite is always present, whether the problem be doctrinal (as in the writings on grace), polemic (as in the *Provinciales* and in other texts linked with the struggle against the Jesuits), or apologetic (as in most of the *Pensées*). Pascal makes his way sound simple, and so it is—for him.

The Unity of Pascal's Thought

Toward a Synoptic View

This introduction to Pascal's thought goes beyond the consideration that Pascal often receives at the hands of literary scholars, because he is clearly more than a literary figure.[1] (In fact it is safe to say that he never believed himself to be engaged in "literature" at all: that is a category that we impose on his work.) It is introductory in two senses. It presents in a summary fashion many of Pascal's concerns and opinions, with some explanation of how he came to have them and how he justified them. My hope is that it will "introduce" in another sense, that it will help the reader to deal directly and fruitfully with Pascal's thought as it is expressed in the works. In these concluding pages I wish to pursue both these aims on a more general level than before. For we can now begin to grasp the shape and meaning of his total enterprise.

There are, of course, other writings of Pascal that we have not discussed or mentioned, except perhaps in passing, such as those ordinarily referred to as his *opuscules*, or what remains—and that is scanty—of his correspondence. The limits set for this volume do not leave space for detailed study of these other texts, but I have included short analyses of them in chapter 7, and I shall here allude to several of them as we go along, so that their relevance to the general design may be seen.

Three notions or terms will be useful as we reflect on the wide range of problems that engaged Pascal's restless mind. In his writings we can usually locate them in one guise or another and trace out their effects. First, there is the subject matter: what he is talking about or inquiring into. Second, the method: the line of thought, the sequence of reasoning he follows as he studies his subject matter. Third, the principle (or principles): what he takes as the point (or points) of departure for his arguments. One of the consequences of the fact that Pascal is an artist and thinker who prizes consistency is

96

that these three aspects are always closely related—so much so that we ordinarily do not feel a need to distinguish them clearly, unless our purpose is, as here, systematic analysis, comparison, and contrast.

Subject Matters: The Objects of Attention

Let us recall briefly some typical works of Pascal with an eye to their mode of presentation, say the *Traité du triangle arithmétique*, the *Traité de l'équilibre des liqueurs*, the *Provinciales*, the *Ecrits sur la grâce*, the *Pensées*, and the *Abrégé de la vie de Jésus-Christ*. The striking diversity of contours and structures that we meet in these works causes us to suspect at once that Pascal's approach—mode of thought and discourse—must vary according to the problems encountered in the subject matters he is treating. He is not an idealist; he does not take for granted that the human mind can by inspecting its own acts and products arrive at an adequate account of what is. (This is one of the convictions that separate him from Descartes and his disciples.) Ideas and methods do not, as Pascal defines and works with them, have priority over things and their properties. In each case the mind must submit to reality and establish a proper relationship to the things under consideration and their special characteristics. The trouble with the theory of the *horreur du vide* was precisely that it attributed to inanimate nature feelings and operations that belong only to creatures or observers that are alive and sentient. Or, for another and more general example on the same point: one of the most important features in the thought of Pascal is the tension he finds between the finite and the infinite; and this tension exists because the finite mind insists on trying to dilate its capacities so as to grasp the nature of something that exceeds it. When one conceives of the infinite as a personal God (as Pascal does), to use human language in speaking of him is a gross error except in the kind of expressions that are sanctioned by the Bible. Everywhere the mind of Pascal is measured by the subject matter at hand, and not the reverse.

Then the question arises: what are, in Pascal's universe, the objects that present themselves to us to be known? The fundamental answer seems to be twofold: things and a book, nature and Scripture. But these terms are opaque until we analyze them. (1) On the side of things and nature we encounter first a Pascalian version of the traditional dualism that divides *bodies* from *souls* (*corps* from *âmes*); then, in those places where Pascal indicates the aspects of souls that interest him most, we see that he must distinguish between the *mind* and the *heart* (*esprit* and *coeur*), broadly understood as the power of knowing and the power of willing; and finally, to the foregoing we must add *quantity* (or *quantities*). Such are the constituent elements, the ultimate furniture of the created world. They are *in nature*, but—and this qualification is necessary if we are to preserve Pascal's instinctive realism—they also *have natures*, so that they hold out to us and to our powers of knowing distinct objects that must be grasped in specific ways. (2) On the side of Scripture, and as though emerging from its depths, all of the preceding entities reappear, but this time *plus God*, and therefore locked in a perspective that is regulated from a transcendental viewpoint.

Even quantity is there: do we not read in the Book of Wisdom (11:21, as cited by Pascal in *De l'Esprit géométrique*) that *Deus fecit omnia in pondere, in numero et mensura?* God made everything in weight (or bodily mass, as Pascal interprets it), in number and measure (or space, as he interprets it); and these three imply each other. The scriptural perspective can never be reduced to the purely natural view, though there is a certain parallelism due to the play of the notion of the infinite. In nature particular things are situated as points or placeholders on infinite scales of number, size, and movement; and in Scripture everything given in nature—including the quantitative infinites—is posed in the presence of a God who is infinite in his mysterious, nonquantitative way.

Methods: The Lines of Thought

If such are the objects to be known, to be put in order, to be integrated into our existence (for one of those bodies and one of those souls go to make up each of us as a self facing out on everything else), what are the methods or investigative sequences required of us by the subject matters as we seek in them the truth and the happiness that we cannot fail to desire? First of all there is a way of thinking that Pascal never seems to forget even when appearing to set it aside (it remains as a term of reference): the method of geometrical demonstration. He expresses the insight that underlies this method in his letter of reply to Père Noël on the subject of the *vide*. One must never, he says, proceed to the act of judging—whether affirmatively or negatively—unless one of two conditions is met: either (1) the judgment is so clear and distinct in itself that it cannot be doubted or (2) it may be deduced from such a self-evident principle. In the treatment of particular problems this intuition leads to an insistence on working with univocal and explicit definitions, with axioms of the kind just mentioned and with their indubitable consequences. Pascal applies the method in the study of quantity, and according as the quantity investigated is continuous or discrete, it eventuates in the sciences of geometry and arithmetic.

However, it is qualified by another distinction. Geometry and arithmetic treat quantities in isolation from things: they use the method on abstract subject matters. It may also be applied concretely, and that is exactly what Pascal does in the treatises and related works that deal with the behavior of liquids and the pressure of the atmosphere—and also in the calculation of probabilities, that paradoxical science of chance (*aleae geometria*), by means of which we succeed in importing something of mathematical rigor and certainty into thinking about future events, which would seem to be irremediably uncertain. In these matters Pascal has transformed the technique of geometrical demonstration into a technique that is empiriometrical, in the sense that it brings observed experience under an order that is formally mathematical. (From the point of view of etymology he returns geometry to its original function: the measurement of the earth.)

But Pascal cares a great deal about a domain more complicated than that of quantities, bodies, and events; and not just more complicated; it is radically different. He would like to consider simultaneously God and the whole scale of realities of which nature is composed—bodies, souls, hearts, minds, and quantities, especially in so far as they enter into the composition of man and into human life. This new field of investigation and the problems encountered there require a new mode of thought and language. Before, in his geometrical, arithmetical, and empiriometrical inquiries, Pascal inspected objects as they are, as they present and assert themselves: his logic was analytical. Now he wishes to look beyond each object to the systematic connections it has with everything else and above all with a transcendent God: his logic becomes relational, synoptic. The basic question is not to formulate the invariable properties of quantities and bodies, but to indicate and perhaps then surmount metaphysical disproportions and to bring about a moral conversion. Undeniable axioms, definitions fixed in advance or known by their own self-certifying light, propositions disposed in a strictly sequential order are impossible. And it is not hard to see why. Those elements and those constructions have as their aim to exclude contradictions—and even the possibility of contradictions—from the outset of the inquiry. To proceed thus in a perspective that centers on God would entail an arbitrary deformation of the subject matter and foreclose forever any chance of understanding it. I mean that, in order to take into account the contradictions inherent in human nature, in order to establish the infinite distance between man and God, and then, in order to resolve the problems thus posed, Pascal is obliged to opt for a dialectical method. (Moreover, moral conversions do not occur according to the laws of geometry; they involve love, and love will not be coerced by reasons.)

Pascalian dialectic occurs in its complete form in the *Pensées*, though one often finds it in other places, where it is not so fully elaborated or is oriented in slightly different directions. To understand it one must distinguish between what I have called its negative and its positive phases. In the former he identifies, develops, and on occasion orchestrates brilliantly contrarieties and paradoxes that he locates in his subject matter, leaving his reader disconcerted, unable to proceed. The logical motion here is nicely summed up in Pascal's phrase, "renversement continuel du pour au contre."[2] The positive phase or *régime* emerges at the moment when Pascal introduces a comprehensive term with reference to which the paradoxes and antitheses yield their authentic sense and become partial expressions of a total truth: this phase completes the first by a continual reconciliation of the *pour* and the *contre*. Excellent examples of the negative side of an argument may be seen in the *Entretien avec M. de Sacy* (the opposition between Montaigne and Epictetus), in the *Provinciales* (the Molinists versus the Calvinists; this opposition recurs many times in the implacably reasoned *Ecrits sur la grâce*), and of course in the *Pensées* (the *misère* versus the *grandeur* of man, the infinites of *grandeur* and *petitesse*). Examples of the positive moment may be seen with special clarity in the *Provinciales* and in the *Ecrits sur la grâce*, where St. Augustine and his views resolve all the conflicts, and in the *Pensées*, where God and Jesus Christ serve constantly as reconciling principles.

However, this bipolar strategy, being essentially *logical*, requires in order to be complete, to be flexible, and simply to have a field of action and deployment, a system of levels or "ordres," which is at once metaphysical, since it lays out the fundamental divisions of reality, and moral, since it sets the stages of an itinerary that stretches

out before each of us. Here we come back to the ensemble of objects
to which methodical thought addresses itself: bodies, minds, quantities
(a domain that is now associated with the mind), and hearts, plus
God; and all these factors are arranged on a hierarchical scale.

Of course the lines are not always so neatly drawn. In the correspondence with the Roannez or in the text "Sur la conversion du
pécheur" Pascal distinguishes between the "monde" of appetites, of
tempting apparent goods, of ceaseless change and the order of real,
invisible, unchanging goods, headed by God; or in the *Lettre* to Queen
Christina of Sweden he contrasts the order of political power and
sovereignty with that of intellectual distinction and truth (Christina's
prodigious achievement is to embody them both); or again, in the
Provinciales, where Pascal repeatedly points out to his adversaries
that their arguments and tactics belong to the realm of coercive force
and can have no effect on issues of intangible (but no less real for
that) truth. These variations all fit, I believe, into the general pattern
of Pascal's dialectic. His way of posing and treating questions engages
us in a dynamic inquiry that subjects us constantly to two tendencies,
distinct but concordant, one of which propels us from the negative to
the positive, while the other invites us to leave the lower for the
higher; and both draw us upward from contradictions and multiplicity
toward unity.

But it is obvious that the *Pensées* include not only an ensemble of
distinctions concerning method and the personal reflection that flows
from and supports them. Pascal is preparing a defense of the Christian
religion; he sees himself as someone who not only has the truth but
also has a vocation to communicate it to others. This interpersonal
framework, though noticeable in many works and passages of works
(see the letters to Père Noël, the *Provinciales*, the *Ecrits sur la
grâce*, the *Discours sur la condition des grands*, and others') is very
clear in the *Pensées*. There Pascal recognizes and defines the elements
that will come into play: the mind and heart, and the character and
social status of his reader as well; he has something like a theory
of assent, of the stages by which it is reached, and of the precise ad-
justments needed according to whether the truth to be conveyed concerns natural or divine subject matters. In the various aspects of this
program we discern the data of a rhetoric, another method that we
must add to Pascal's repertory. In the seventeenth century his talents
in this discipline were acknowledged: we read in a footnote in the
second edition of the *Art de penser* or logic of Port-Royal that "the

late Mr. Pascal knew as much genuine rhetoric as anyone has ever known."

Here there is a point to be underscored: for Pascal rhetoric is not an autonomous discipline. With him we are far from the eclectic and pragmatic attitude of Cicero, who practiced rhetoric as a universal art capable of discriminating in any situation between what is valid and valuable and what is not, and capable also of finding ways to communicate effectively the wisdom thus obtained. (Many writers and theorists in seventeenth-century France held this view—Patru, Balzac, and Rapin come to mind.) Nor do we see in Pascal anything of the Aristotelian notion, according to which rhetoric is an independent discipline once its proper subject matter—questions that cannot be investigated or decided scientifically—has been identified. Pascal belongs rather to the spiritual family of St. Augustine and Plato, who accord a place to rhetoric provided it is made to depend strictly on truth (best written with a capital T) that is known by ways and means that are nonrhetorical. The rhetoric that we encounter in the *Pensées*, in the letters to the Roannez, in the letter on the death of his father, in the *Ecrits sur la grâce* (to mention some outstanding examples) is therefore an adaptation and a prolongation of Pascal's dialectic. He understood quite well, it seems, the other possibility, that of a technique of persuasion detached from the truth: is that not what he saw in the manuals and in the conduct of the Jesuit casuists? Their obliging attitude toward those who consulted them, their "probable opinions," their mode of reasoning form in a sense the negative counterpart of that "véritable rhétorique" for which Pascal was known. As for the interpenetration of rhetoric and dialectic, it is so marked that often one should no doubt speak of a single process having two aspects; and the stages of the journey through which Pascal's reader must pass—the principal points along the line of assent—correspond to the phases and articulations of the dialectical scheme.

Actually the question of rhetoric in Pascal's thought is somewhat more complex than the foregoing remarks might lead one to suppose. Perhaps it is best to think of him as recognizing three species of this discipline: (1) the version that is based on theology dialectically conceived, which I have associated with the *Pensées* and related texts; (2) the version that is essentially an "art d'agréer," which I have attributed to the Jesuits, an art of pleasing and influencing apart from strict considerations of truth; and (3) the version that is an extension of geometrical reasoning. Pascal outlines this last in the fragmentary texts on the "esprit géométrique," where he telescopes the technique of persuasion and that of demonstration into one. The resulting "art de persuader" adopts rules of self-evidence, of definition, and of reasoning that are indistinguishable from those of geometry. Many devices and lines of argument in the *Provinciales* exemplify this approach. So there is justification for saying that Pascal envisages three kinds of rhetoric and that he utilizes two of them while excluding the third because of its indifference regarding truth.

Principles: The Points of Departure

Pascal exploits, then, the possibilities in various methods; and they change according to the nature and complexity of the object to which he directs his attention. But these methods, whose essential function is to create orderly sequences of ideas and words, can work only with the aid of principles, of starting points that allow the methods to take hold of their characteristic objects. And the diversity of these principles helps us to understand the technical flexibility and ingenuity of Pascal. The significance of what I am saying will become clear if I suggest some examples and applications.

(1) The mathematical method of Pascal is oriented toward *construction*. It starts with simple, indivisible elements—rather like building blocks—that can be assembled, by the use of explicit rules of combination, into coherent composites. Thus the works of geometry, arithmetic, and empiriometric science are based on the aspects (or elements) of quantity and things that are matched with the original definitions. Basing itself on such principles, his method proceeds to create in a verbal construction a series of demonstrations that reflect the natures and the properties of the known objects.

(2) The dialectical method is oriented toward *unification*. Whereas in mathematical reasoning the principles (and one should no doubt add: the rules of combination) are identified *in advance* and are known in all their self-evidence from the outset of the discourse, in Pascal's dialectic one does not reach a truly clear intuition of the principle until the end, after the reconciliation of the themes and anti-themes that served to fix the context of the discussion. Nature is contradictory: it stretches endlessly in the two directions of largeness and smallness. Man is contradictory: he has his vanity and his nobility, his incomplete truths and inadequate goods that can only disappoint his thirst for total and infinite satisfaction. The Bible is

contradictory: the two Testaments, taken literally, do not present a coherent story. But the two infinites of nature are united in God; pride and concupiscence are reoriented and harmonized by Christian morality and divine grace, and all human aspirations will be fulfilled by the saturating Truth and Goodness of God; and the parts of the Bible, when interpreted correctly, have a single center in Jesus Christ, that is, in God. It is possible to find intermediate principles of syn-thesis in Pascal's dialectical thought, but the final and overarching principle is always the same.

(3) The rhetoric of Pascal in its most characteristic use is oriented toward *conversion*, and consequently toward the search for means leading to that end. Whereas in geometry he expresses his principles at the beginning of his proofs, and in dialectic he finds them at the end of his inquiry, here he concentrates his attention *in medias res*: he discerns and deploys his principles in the course of his argument. The presupposed end is an act of belief requiring a particular disposition of the human heart and mind; the principles present themselves as the means of producing that disposition. Pascal knows exactly what they are and in what order they normally become perti-nent (though deviations from this order are not ruled out): "Il y a trois moyens de croire, la raison, la coutume, l'inspiration."[3] Reasons and proofs for the mind, new habits for the heart (and more broadly, for the whole *machine*), and then, from a higher order, a gift.

Interrelations

I have emphasized distinctions to be noted in the methods Pascal uses, and I think that they do indeed tend to become more and more differentiated as they are worked out in application to specific prob-lems. However, one often finds, alongside the methodological ten-dency that predominates in a particular text, traces or episodes that belong properly to one of the others. For example, at the end of the treatise on the summation of numerical powers, conceived in the framework of the deductive method, Pascal invokes a comprehensive or dialectical principle—Nature as a lover of unity ("unitatis amatrix natura")—that leads him to the possibility of unifying two domains apparently quite distinct: the measurement of continuous magnitudes in geometry and the addition of numerical powers. Or, in the *Pensées*, where he is already combining the energies of dialectic and rhetoric, should we not see in the argument of the *pari* an episode borrowed from the demonstrative mode of geometry (in the broad sense of that term)? And several readers of Pascal have compared the scheme of the three moral and metaphysical orders, carefully separated and yet linked by numerous analogies, to the numerical orders and to the orders of geometrical figures.

In spite of these examples of local cooperation I believe that we are obliged to say that the differences between Pascal's methods remain essentially intact. Of course that does not prevent him from establishing among them some important general correlations or from having among his "idées de derrière la tête" a kind of table. I would sum up the situation hypothetically as follows. To the three fundamental realities—corporeal, intellectual, spiritual—correspond three faculties of knowing—sense, mind, and heart. The mind, when it is working in its own domain, which is *par excellence* that of quantity, adopts a procedure that is axiomatic, propositional, and linear, in short, the method of *geometry*. It may also turn down toward bodies and sense experience and there engage in a *mathesis* of the observable. The heart, aided by reason but having reasons of its own, seems to be at once a target and a source of *rhetoric*; it expresses itself in developments that are affective, intuitive, digressive. And those "digressions sur chaque point qui a rapport à la fin, pour la montrer toujours," which characterize the order of the heart, lead naturally to the intuitions and devices of a powerful *dialectic.*

By its nature this last method has an architectonic function; it knows how to detect the presence and the workings of principles at all levels. For example, Pascal may be certain in his heart of the truth of principles like space and number; and then, by a descending movement, he reaches the plane of the mind where the two notions are elaborated in the sciences of geometry and arithmetic; he may then pass to the level of bodies, where the notions are specified anew in data obtained by experimentation. Or, in morality, by an opposite movement his reflection may turn upward: the contradictions he observes in the opinions and actions of carnal men open the way to the "raisons des effets"—to pride and concupiscence; but they are intermediate principles, the true explanation being found only on the level of heart and in the mystery of original sin. Perhaps at this point we should make explicit a fourth "order" or degree to be added to the other three—that of the transcendent (and partly hidden) God who is the beginning and the end of everything.

When we think of the methodological pluralism of Pascal in this fashion, we are not dealing with a simple addition of disparate factors. It is rather an ensemble of techniques that reinforce and sustain each other; and Pascal seems to have concluded that if the seeker after knowledge or happiness respects their diversity, their proper requirements, their peculiar modes of operation, he will succeed in adapting his search to the varying facets of reality and to the distinctive principles that make it intelligible and accessible.

More Interrelations

I should like to propose finally some remarks based not on the scheme of the three orders but on the neutral terms with which I began. By specifying them further we may reach a truly fundamental level of analysis and of general insight.

As for *method*, there is an interesting fragment in the *Pensées* that points the way to a clear statement of what I wish to say.

> Pyrrh.
> J'écrirai ici mes pensées sans ordre et non pas peut-être dans une confusion sans dessein. C'est le véritable ordre et qui marquera toujours mon objet par le désordre même. (578; fr, 532)[4]

Even in this sort of spontaneous self-expression, here attached to Pyrrhonian skepticism, Pascal has and sees a purpose. This confusion has, after all, a certain unity and coherence because it proceeds from one and the same writing subject. This use of words is regulated by *grammar*; it stands in contrast to the other arts or methods favored by Pascal, since the discourse that results has a unity that is almost purely additive: one expressed thought plus another expressed thought plus another, and so on. As I see it, this is the lowest degree of coherence in a scale that (by coincidence or design or both) Pascal fills out completely by means of the methods that I have just analyzed in some detail.

Beyond this unintended kind of sequence we pass to another degree of coherence when Pascal introduces into the situation a second person, whose role is that of an addressee or interlocutor. Then a tighter kind of order, belonging to the art of *rhetoric*, becomes appropriate. It takes into account the inconstant thoughts and feelings of the reader or listener; its procedure is informal and subject to digressions, though the end of the process never gets out of sight. One way of controlling and strengthening the capabilities of this rhetoric consists in making it depend on modes of thinking and writing that are still more highly disciplined. The next degree on the scale, that of *dialectic*, goes beyond rhetoric in rigor and sequential movement. It requires a definite progression from negative to positive in modes of statement, and from lower to higher in levels of being and action; but its movement is retrospective—if not, indeed, circular—in that at any moment a telegraphic formula or table may lay out both sides of a question and indicate the answer to it. Next and finally comes the technical coherence that Pascal admires in *geometry*, with its infallible progressions of principles and consequents. (And it will be recalled that the non-dialectical species of rhetoric may take into itself elements of this procedure.) If we start, therefore, with questions of method, we see that Pascal's works oblige us to make distinctions and that the distinctions give us modes of discourse covering the scale of coherence from the loosest and most familiar to the tightest and furthest removed from ordinary experience.

As for *principles*, Pascal must select, as I have suggested above, principles or starting points that will give him access to the properties of the things to be studied. In geometry, arithmetic, and physics he concentrates on elements or on particular readings taken from measuring instruments—on least parts that can be put together for systematic understanding and treatment; in dealing with philosophical and theological questions he rises easily to a great panoramic view that joins finite and infinite being into an orderly whole, and then he shows in leisurely detail how finite creatures (especially man) depend on their infinite creator. When he shifts into the rhetorical vein, ends and means control the discussion; he connects thought (as reasoning, as proofs) with its intended consequences in action, whether he is denouncing the false productions of the Jesuit fathers or fostering the intellectual and moral dispositions that prepare for faith. In the remarks (that I quoted earlier) on writing down what one thinks in its pristine confusion and in many other less "Pyrrhonian" passages, he takes up with perfect assurance and illuminating results the two aspects of expression: thought and words. Taken in themselves the principles furnish a wide and promising assortment of points of departure; taken in conjunction with the methods, they lead at once into characteristic lines of thought: elements into geometry, wholes into dialectic, means into rhetoric, and expressions into grammar.

As for *subject matters*, Pascal covers an encyclopedic range: Scripture and nature (or God and creation), bodies and quantities, minds and hearts. Not only does that list include all the furniture of the universe; it also pulls the various items into complementary relationships, since each pair sets up an exhaustive opposition. That these realities—natural, human, divine—lend themselves to fruitful treatment according to the principles and methods that Pascal brings to bear on them is attested by the impressive canon of Pascal's works.

Of course there is much in that canon that was never fully realized—for many reasons, some of them beyond Pascal's control. Still, what Pascal achieved is extraordinary in its scope, power, and proven vitality. And perhaps a reading such as that proposed here can point the way to a perfection more fundamental than formal completeness. Through the artistic and intellectual strands that underlie the works and through the mental habits of which those strands are symptoms we may know something of the intense, mobile, sovereign energy that directs the thought of Pascal.

Chapter Six

The Continuing
Presence of Pascal

Pascal and Some of his Contemporaries

After studying Pascal's achievements in themselves, let us now consider them in relation to the intellectual milieu in which they appeared and also in relation to the reactions of readers since the seventeenth century. Let us try to do this in such a way as to throw light on the significance and influence of the works without undermining them, without explaining them away by references to overriding factors of history or expectations of readers.

By the force of circumstance Pascal came into contact with the best scientific thought of his time. The fact that his father belonged to the Académie Mersenne had as a consequence that young Blaise was introduced at an early age into this circle of first-rate minds. They were at the center of European work in mathematics, physics, and scientific epistemology. Directly or indirectly they knew the work of Galileo, Torricelli, Hobbes, Descartes, Fermat. They were not professional scientists as we know them today; they were, rather, brilliant amateurs working in a competitive atmosphere, each one eager to bring his latest "invention" to the group and to discuss it in the growing, rapidly evolving context of scientific inquiry.

Pascal appears to have felt immediately at home in this situation. He saw what problems were *à la mode* and undertook to make his contribution to solving them. He did remarkable new work on conic sections, a subject of much interest at the time, not only in pure mathematics but also in physics, where Kepler and Galileo were showing that the motions of planets and falling bodies could be interpreted in the light of figures such as ellipses and parabolas. He was one of the founders of the new science of projective geometry. In his work on the measurements of the cycloid curve he came close to the invention of the integral calculus. With Fermat he founded the theory of probability calculations. In the field we know as mechanical computation he invented and produced in some quantity a workable machine for carrying out the fundamental operations of arithmetic. If he did not leave a large body of completed works in mathematics, he was nevertheless an extraordinarily lucid and innovative thinker on several important fronts. His contributions inspired others (Leibniz, for example), and opened the way for more finished accounts by his successors. Geometry, with its visual equipment of points, lines, and curves, suited Pascal's imagination especially well. He saw less clearly, it would seem, the importance and the possibilities of algebra: there Descartes was supreme.

In physics, too, the work of Pascal stands in contrast to that of Descartes. Both saw that the future belonged to a physics that was mathematical in its mode of statement and explanation, but they proceeded with vastly different emphases. Descartes was the system-builder who sought a universal view of nature formed out of clear and certain ideas; Pascal was the problematic thinker who studied particular difficulties and looked for solutions fitting the cases at hand. He worked empirically and experimentally, whereas Descartes preferred a basically deductive procedure (though one should not underestimate the amount of systematic observation done by Descartes). A further point: Galileo—and later Newton—were fascinated by moving bodies and the laws of their motions; with Pascal the fascination lay rather in bodies that move toward rest in equilibrium.

Although he cared a great deal about science and invested much time in it, Pascal became increasingly convinced that abstract and external objects of knowledge (as found in mathematics and physics) are not relevant to man. Perhaps this is a reflection of his frequent insistence on the need for a "proportion" or likeness between knower and object known. In any case, the science proper to man is reflexive and unique; it is, quite simply, the science of man. Here he parts company with many of his scientifically minded contemporaries; and, again, the contrast with Descartes is sharp. In the Cartesian view all sciences—whether mathematical, natural, or human—constitute a seamless fabric of truths, generated and held together by a single method (the model being geometry).

Thanks to two clear and distinct ideas Descartes knows that man is a composite of body and mind, and he proceeds to study both of those substances in the same analytical way. The body is a machine that occupies space; as an ensemble of interacting pieces it serves almost as a model for the soul and its interacting powers (though the soul has, of course, no extent). The heart is a physical organ that heats the blood and by making it expand causes it to circulate. The passions, which Descartes defines as motions in the soul, are analyzed, combined, and catalogued as so many separate items of psychic activity. Pascal accepts the mechanical ideas and imagery for the body, but he extends them regularly to the unconscious functioning of the mind and to the working of habit in general. What was, apparently, an unintended analogy in Descartes is developed literally by Pascal. Where Descartes derives more and more passions from the half-dozen that he takes as "primitive" or primary, Pascal tends to move in just the opposite direction; he may speak of passions in the plural, but the essential thing is to see them as coming from a single source: concupiscence. As we have often noted, the heart, instead of being a physical reality for Pascal, is the core of the person, the seat of desire and of charity. It is also a power of knowing and, in fact, it knows the most important things of all—in science, the first principles, and in moral life, God.

Pascal's conception of man cannot be separated from his defense of the Christian religion. In this field, by virtue of his deep insight, his passion for clarity and consistency, his mastery of language, and by his boldness he stands far above the numerous contemporaries who wrote apologetic works. Among the lines of argument that he encountered two may be mentioned here. Starting from the beauties and order of external nature, deists reasoned back to the existence of a providential God. Pascal rejects this path, for it does not lead to a true conversion and to the God of the Old and New Testaments; nor does it have lasting effect on any except those who believe already. The obvious alternative is to start immediately from grounds in faith and Scripture; but Pascal rejects this also. That is the usual route followed by those who base their arguments on the practice of religion—and Pascal appears to think that for the kind of audience he has in mind such a case has ceased to be convincing. Actually, he combines in his particular synthesis both natural and supernatural arguments: both kinds have their place, provided they are used in the right senses and in the right order. He argues first from nature— but from human nature, not nature in general; he brings in Scripture only after the reader is ready for it (as we saw at the end of the *pari*); and, again, his appeal to it is highly selective, since he reads it as confirming his description of the human situation and as a source of certainty regarding the coming of a Redeemer. Moreover, Pascal has a strong sense of the limits of argumentation. His notion of belief leaves essential roles to be played by habit and inspiration. One may say that the doctrinal basis for all of this is Augustinian and Jansenist; and that is of course correct. However, Pascal did not try to innovate in such matters of substance. He saw his contribution in another way: "Let it not be said," he remarks in fragment 696, "that I have said nothing new; the disposition of the material is new; in playing tennis both players use the same ball, but one places it better."

Although it is certain that Pascal did not think of himself as a literary figure, we usually place him in the company of the great seventeenth-century French writers, and especially with the moralists. He has an eye for moral explanations, for *raisons des effets*, as he calls them, that suggests the reductive views expressed by La Rochefoucauld, who liked to see in our virtues disguised forms of our vices, and more than anything else, of self-love. This pervasive *amour-propre* is to La Rochefoucauld what *concupiscence* is to Pascal. But if the diagnosis of human failings is very similar in the *Maximes* (1665) and in the *Pensées*, the remedies differ completely. La Rochefoucauld proposes *honnêteté*, tact, and sociability, so that we can live together peaceably and pleasantly; Pascal believes all that to be mere decoration: for a true transformation of self he proposes humility, penitence, and grace.

Pascal studies society, as La Bruyère was to do after him in *Les Caractères* (1688). La Bruyère observes, defines, portrays; he gives back to society, he says in his preface, what it has lent him. Pascal is much less inclined to describe and picture social reality; he generalizes and looks for the hidden principle in what he observes, and that turns out to be force, not justice. La Bruyère can be quite critical; he often laments the fact that personal merit goes unnoticed and unrewarded at the court, in Paris, and elsewhere; but his essentially conservative view of society as a more or less self-contained hierarchy directed by a divinely appointed ruler lacks the opening onto the infinite that characterizes Pascal's thought here as in mathematics and physics. Human justice, though admirable for him when it preserves civil peace, is radically overshadowed by divine justice.

Pascal has also some of the excellences found in the classical theater (he would not have appreciated this judgment, for he agreed with his friend Nicole in considering the theater to be bad for morals). Like Molière he has a dramatic imagination, a gift for dialogue, a talent for seeing the gesture or finding the word that reveals at a stroke the depths of human vanity. Like the Racine of the later plays, he knows that life, if it is to have meaning, must be referred to immortal or supernatural wills and to a hereafter; and tragedy befalls those who fail to take all the dimensions of moral reality into account and in the proper order.

A Sampler of Judgments

The scientific works of Pascal have tended to be the province of specialists. As contributions to knowledge they have taken their place in the evolving fabric of mathematics and physics. If in some ways they have been superseded, they have never lost their values as models; in design, manner of reasoning, expression, and in experimental inventiveness they have had a constant appeal for scientists and historians of ideas. As one might expect, the *Provinciales* and the *Pensées* have interested a broader spectrum of readers. Indeed, in the reactions and interpretations of those readers they have had a fascinating life, a life that tells us much not only about the works themselves and their potentialities but also about the changing concerns of successive generations.

Of course the letters had their detractors in the seventeenth century. Annat, to whom two of them were addressed, accused the anonymous author of a lack of conscience and respect; he suggested that Port-Royal give him a change of assignment and set him to writing comedies and farces—a judgment typical of Jesuit opinion. But the *Provinciales* had their strong admirers. Mme de Sévigné loved the "petites lettres." Boileau, always a strong partisan of the ancients in any discussion of literary works, made one exception here; he considered the letters to be the most perfect prose work in the French language, and, indeed, to be superior to anything of their kind ancient or modern. Charles Perrault, always a strong partisan of the moderns, composed an encyclopedic survey (in his *Parallèle des anciens et des modernes*, 1690) of ancient and modern accomplishments in the arts and sciences; for him, as for Boileau, the *Provinciales* were unique, remarkable for purity of language, nobility of thought, solidity in reasoning, *finesse* in mockery and satire, and for attractiveness of a rare kind throughout. Racine explains Pascal's success in this venture by the fact that to the treatment of matters usually left to theologians he brought his own marvelous vivacity and charm.

Voltaire admires the letters as containing all kinds of eloquence; and, in particular, as combining unexpectedly *éloquence* and *plaisanterie* (a noun based on the verb *plaisanter*, which has a range of meanings from good-humored joking to serious mockery). The first letters remind him of the best comedies of Molière; the last ones have an elevation not exceeded by Bossuet (the greatest preacher of his age). Condorcet, who edited Pascal's *Pensées* in 1776, prefaced it with a eulogy in which he takes up once more Voltaire's terms. He finds in the alliance of satire and serious eloquence the secret of the success of the *Letters*. That was what made of them a book for all sorts and conditions of readers, for all minds, for all ages.

Early in the nineteenth century Chateaubriand noted again the effect of the *Provinciales* on the process of perfecting the French language. They set a model of usage for Bossuet and Racine, and also a model of perfect *plaisanterie* and of strong reasoning; but in 1831 he criticized Pascal for taking away the moral force of the Jesuits, for being "only a slanderer of genius," who had left us "an immortal lie."

The opinions of Joseph de Maistre and of Michelet show further how the *Provinciales* became engaged in nineteenth-century passions and ideologies. De Maistre, who has been called "a Voltaire turned inside out," lived through the French Revolution and came out of it an ultraroyalist and a strong supporter of the church and the pope. He detested the "heresy" of Jansenism and, therefore, the *Provinciales* of Pascal. The work has, in his view (expressed in 1821), some good features, but they are spoiled by the monotony of the outline and the dialogue; it is a witty libel, full of bitterness and hatred. Michelet, who had no use for the Jesuits and for whom the key to the history of France lay in the struggle of its people against despotism, thought that the Jansenists, whether or not they exaggerated the doctrine of grace, were "the party of virtue." Rather than going too far against their adversaries, Arnauld and Pascal had held back deliberately because they did not want to undermine the ideas and practices of confession and spiritual counseling.

In his *Port-Royal* (1840) Sainte-Beuve evokes another image of Pascal, that of the reader of Montaigne and the man of the world who brought into a theological debate new notes of humor, playfulness, and a certain fashionable indifference. Pascal defined in fact an attitude that would be taken up by a long line of commentators on Jesuits, Molinists, Thomists—and other religious thinkers, and for less edifying purposes than those of Pascal. Building, it would seem, on Voltaire's remark about the different qualities of the first and last letters, Sainte-Beuve draws attention in the first ten to an art of ironic dialogue akin to that of Plato; and in letters 11 through 16, he discerns more than once, he says, the art of the great orators of antiquity, Cicero and Demosthenes, and especially the latter.

In the twentieth century we seem to have reached a degree of serenity in views concerning the substance of the *Provinciales* (there are exceptions: the Abbé Bremond, who had been a Jesuit, never completely forgave them). Attention tends to fall less on details, on the surprising probable opinions, or on the abuses of casuistry than on the general validity of Pascal's argument. That a deviation from morality based on the Gospel and on the writings of the church fathers did occur in the thinking and practice of certain casuists is historically true; and it can be agreed among those who must deal technically with such matters that Pascal diagnosed the situation correctly and proposed a sound remedy for it (even if he was not exempt in what he said from simplifications and excesses). Style and, in general, the use of language in the letters continue to interest scholars and critics. The literary historian Gustave Lanson has studied Pascal's lively but logical sentence-forms and his un-Scholastic rhetoric in his *Art de la prose* (1908). One of his successors, Antoine Adam, in his *Histoire de la littérature française au XVIIᵉ siècle* (1951), stresses in his turn the untraditional character of Pascal's approach to problems of persuasive discourse, taking as his cue a sentence from the *Pensées* where reliance on rules is condemned and true eloquence put above the academic kind: "La vraie éloquence se moque de l'éloquence." More recently analyses based on concepts and devices borrowed from linguistics and even from treatises on rhetoric have achieved considerable precision in describing the rhetorical situations found in the *Provinciales* and Pascal's use of language within those frameworks.

In the seventeenth century the *Pensées* were not so well known as the *Provinciales*. Mme de Sévigné, for us the model contemporary reader, referred more often in her correspondence to the letters than to the *Pensées*, though she found the latter "solid" and "useful" for reflections on our common anxieties, on our unstable inclinations, on our need to accommodate ourselves to conditions in our lives that we cannot change. The eighteenth-century figure most affected by Pascal was almost certainly Voltaire—in the sense that he saw in the *Pensées* a challenge to which he must respond directly. He admits that Pascal is a "giant," and a "conquerer of minds"; unfortunately those rare merits are not joined to "true philosophy." In the twenty-fifth and final letter of his *Lettres philosophiques* (1734)—actually about Voltaire's experiences in England—he offers a series of comments on selected fragments from the *Pensées*. I dare, he said, to take up the cause of humanity against this sublime misanthrope. He goes at once to the heart of the matter: Pascal's incorrect conception of human nature. Voltaire views man as an ensemble of needs and desires equipped with the instrument of reason so that he may satisfy his wants. Contrary to what Pascal thought, human nature is not torn by inner conflicts; it is what it is and has been. Why should one invent a paradoxical human being and then find oneself obliged to resort to the enigma of original sin in order to make sense of him? Moreover, the mysterious biblical God involved in that story has nothing in common with Voltaire's Supreme Being, who is accessible to reason. Although he was hardly a profound reader of Pascal, Voltaire saw unerringly that no compromise was possible with a moral and religious perspective so different from his own.

D'Alembert, the Encyclopedist, thought the *Provinciales* far superior to the *Pensées*, but hazarded the guess in 1767 that the latter would be more lasting, since Christianity would probably outlast the "humble society" of the Jesuits. Earlier, in the *Discours préliminaire* of the *Encyclopédie* (1751), he praised Pascal as a universal and sublime genius, whose talents had been denied to philosophy—something that could never be regretted enough, except (he added cautiously) for the fact that religion had profited from them. In 1772 Goethe expressed the conviction that "Voltaire, Hume, La Mettrie, Helvétius, Rousseau and their whole school" had done less harm to morality and religion than "that ill and narrow-minded Pascal."

Chateaubriand's *Génie du christianisme* (1802), a preromantic essay in Christian apologetics, contains a glowing tribute to Pascal. It lists his many accomplishments during the thirty-nine years of his life, and concludes by referring to him as a "terrifying genius." Sainte-Beuve is subtler and fairer in his *Histoire de Port-Royal* (1840). He looks systematically for Pascal's fundamental qualities, interpreting him as a personality, as a representation of human understanding facing the universe outside and the self inside, and finding at last the one key: faith in a God who makes himself known to the heart. Stendhal is reported to have said, surprisingly, that when he read Pascal, he seemed to be rereading himself, that of all writers Pascal was the one he resembled most in spirit.

Outside of France Friedrich Schleiermacher, the exponent in Germany of religion as based on insight and feeling apart from dogma, was of the opinion that Pascal was the profoundest of all French thinkers. Nietzsche felt strongly about Pascal, writing on one occasion (others could be mentioned), "I do not read Pascal, I love him" (1888). Kierkegaard, from whom one might have expected a favorable reaction, judged Pascal—and all apologists—severely: "The first Christian to invent the idea of defending Christianity was a new Judas, for he, too, betrayed with a kiss."

Ernest Havet, whose remarkable edition of the *Pensées*—with a commentary that is often excellent—appeared in 1851, added another nuance to the portrait done by Sainte-Beuve, when he called attention to the mark left on Pascal's passionate and geometrical spirit by physical suffering and the threat of death. The work of Havet exemplifies a striking feature of Pascal studies during the latter half of the nineteenth century: the renewal of interest in the manuscripts of the *Pensées* and in the possibility (or rather the necessity) of using them in preparing a satisfactory edition. Of this movement I shall speak below in conclusion.

At the turn of the century (1897) Renouvier, often preoccupied in his philosophical works with the themes of individual liberty and the place of man in the universe, said that Pascal had become something very like a contemporary author ("comme un auteur de notre temps"). That same year William James argued in *The Will to Believe* that when we are faced with options that cannot be decided on rational grounds we have a right to such beliefs as help us lead our lives. He quotes approvingly from the *pari* in developing his views; regarding the mathematical calculations, however, he observes that "if we were ourselves in the place of the Deity, we should probably take particular pleasure in cutting off believers of this pattern from their infinite reward." Bergson credited Pascal in 1905 with having introduced into philosophy a way of thinking that is not based on reason, pure and simple, since he corrects geometry by the workings of the *esprit de finesse,* nor is it dependent on mystical contemplation, since his method leads to confirmable results.

Pascal's little sentence on the eternal (and frightening) silence of infinite space (fragment 201) inspired some negative reflections in the mind of Valéry ("Variation sur une pensée," 1923). Though beautiful as a poem, it is disquieting as an apologetic *pensée*; something impure about it suggests that here and elsewhere Pascal is concerned with the "game of writing"; he wants both heaven and mundane glory. Unamuno (in 1923) attributed to Pascal on the one hand a skeptical, ironic, scientific sense and, on the other, the equivalent of the tragic sense, the hunger for eternity that is characteristic of the Spaniard. Louis de Broglie hit on a formula that seems to fit better than the "effrayant génie" of Chateaubriand when he wrote in 1951, "Pascal, ce fulgurant génie": his adjective calls up the image of something brilliant, flashing, lightninglike.

More recently still other currents have seemed to be latent in the *Pensées*. For the sociologist of literature, Lucien Goldmann, Pascal exemplifies in the structure and movement of his dialectic a stage in the evolution of modern thought toward Hegel, Marx, and doctrines of social revolution. Existentialists have found it possible to link themes such as anxiety, awareness of freedom and radical choices, alienation from the physical universe, and the leap of faith to their analogues in the *Pensées*. Asked in an interview (1959) what writers had helped him become aware of what he wanted to say, Camus mentioned two names, as far as other writers ("les anciens") were concerned: Molière and Pascal. Critics and interpreters who take their principles from the science of language—in its current structuralist or its semiotic guise—have analyzed Pascal's discourse, making discoveries about the genesis of sense in the *Pensées* (as a function of his linguistic habits); and it has even been noted that Pascal himself was a sophisticated critic of discourse.[1]

The Manuscripts and the Copies

It is fitting to add to the foregoing opinions a summary of the revolution that has lately taken place in our knowledge of the texts themselves. For more than a century and a half—from 1670 to 1842, to be exact—editors used as their starting point the first, so-called "Port-Royal" edition, the contents of which they rearranged more or less freely to suit their purposes, and to which they added other fragments as they became available. During this long period the Pascal of the *Pensées* was in effect a prisoner of that edition, incomplete to begin with, amended according to the lights and prudence of the original editors, and ordered according to a plan that made sense to them. Victor Cousin pointed out in 1842 the scandalous fact that although the Pascal manuscripts were in the Bibliothèque nationale in Paris, no one consulted them, not even editors, in spite of the enormous difference existing between the original texts and all editions without exception. He judged it urgently necessary for some one to gather up the materials and to make them known in an accurate form. For almost another century and a half editors have sought to realize his wish. Actually the problem is twofold: (1) to secure a text that is as complete and exact as possible, and (2) to decide on the order in which the fragments are to be presented. Both problems are formidable. The curious thing about what has happened is that by solving the first difficulty researchers and textual critics have apparently solved the second.

There are three main sources for the texts: the "Recueil original," a bound volume or album to the pages of which many (but not all) of Pascal's papers, varying in size, were glued; and then the so-called "first" and "second" copies of the manuscripts. At first, as in the editions of Faugère (1844) and Havet (1852)—but the trend lasted until the end of the century—attention was focused on the "Recueil original." But so many different plans (usually claiming to be faithful to Pascal's intentions) were proposed by editors for the disposition of the texts that a reaction set in. Despairing of ever recovering an authentic order, Gustave Michaut chose in 1896 simply to reproduce "the arbitrary disorder" of the manuscripts in the "Recueil." Léon Brunschvicg, starting from the same basic conviction, but working along a line diametrically opposed, set about arranging the fragments in a "logical continuity" that he determined, though of course he took into account internal and other evidence. His edition, published in 1897, was for a generation accepted as standard, even definitive.

However, a dramatic shift occurred in the fourth and fifth decades of this century. The researches of Zacharie Tourneur and Louis Lafuma (issuing in editions of 1938 and 1948, respectively) brought to light the fact that the "Recueil original" had been constituted in 1710–11, whereas the copies appeared to have been made soon after the death of Pascal in 1662 with the intention of recording the state of his papers at that time. Tourneur and Lafuma took the "Première copie" as their base-text; but, as Philippe Sellier has recently shown in his edition of 1976, there are good reasons for believing that the "Seconde copie" (which has a disposition of the fragments significantly different from that of the first) was the "reference copy" of Gilberte Pascal, used during the preparation of the 1670 edition; and so it probably represents Pascal's last thoughts on the ordering of the texts. That is roughly where the matter stands now. It is apparent that present-day readers are in a better position than any preceding generation to study the structure, the texture, and the significance of this major component in Pascal's total *oeuvre*.

Because of his multifaceted achievements Pascal soon emerged as an imposing figure in his own century, a period when intellectual and artistic activity was taking place on the highest level in many fields. There is also much evidence, some of it alluded to briefly here, that he has stimulated and influenced every generation of readers since his works first appeared, down to the present time, when Pascal studies are in a particularly effervescent state. He has shown himself to be exemplary and inexhaustible.

Chapter Seven

An Afterword on the Shorter Works

The résumés that follow will make it possible for the reader to form an idea of some shorter works on nonscientific subjects that are usually referred to and published as Pascal's *opuscules*. The themes and contents of these works can, in most cases, be linked to the analyses presented in the preceding chapters, though an elaborate treatment of that relation is beyond the scope of this volume.

"Discours sur les passions de l'amour" [Discourse on the passions of love]

The attribution of this document to Pascal is uncertain, as is its date. The manuscript was discovered by Victor Cousin in 1843. The copyist had inscribed on it words to the effect that it was attributed to "M. Pascal," and Cousin considered this attribution to be correct. There has always been opposition to this view, and it has grown stronger in the last half century.[1] The document consists of approximately ten pages of reflections in the form of maxim-like sentences and short paragraphs. It has little in the way of plan or discursive sequence, but certain ideas and images recur, giving it an elusive air of consistency.

Man is born for thought and for pleasure, but he foregoes the happiness that is available in "pure" thought for action and for passions that fill the mind apropos of an object or person. (Note that the discourse is about passions in the plural: love is at the center of a loosely defined group of feelings.) Ambition and love are said to be the main passions, the former being usually, though not always, dominant in the old and the latter in the young. Discussed from the male point of view, love is not divided into species, except perhaps into the weak kind and the strong, obsessive kind (this is the only one that really interests the author). It starts on the basis of our natural tendency to pleasure, and it works out, so to speak, from an innate model of beauty—innate at least in its "premiers rayons," its first glimmerings. To this model the lover compares particular women, not mechanically, but allowing some leeway for divergence from the model. The agreeable and the beautiful are identical. Poets have been wrong in separating thought and lucidity from love: love is not blind; a great and clear mind loves ardently, with a distinct view of the one he loves. The text contains a brief reference to the opposition, familiar in Pascal, between the geometrical mind and the subtle or intuitive mind (the "esprit de géométrie" versus the "esprit de finesse"). The former has slow, hard, and inflexible views; the latter sees actively the various lovable characteristics of the loved person; and when one has both kinds of mind, one enjoys the advantages of both strength and flexibility in the relationship. The course of love is not analyzed in detail: it is there or not, one is near the beloved or not, it is *naissant* or *avancé*—in an early or advanced state. It is basically the same everywhere, but customs and climate cause some differences.

The allusion to the two *esprits* reminds us of course of the *Pensées* (fragments 512–13), as does the idea, here present, of an inner emptiness that man tries to fill by action, novelties, objects of passion: that agrees easily with Pascal's fragments on the human condition and on the role of *divertissement* in our lives. But it is difficult to see Pascal as the author of a sentence like the following: "Qu'une vie est heureuse quand elle commence par l'amour et qu'elle finit par l'ambition! or this: "L'homme est né pour le plaisir: il le sent, il n'en faut point d'autre preuve. Il suit donc sa raison en se donnant au plaisir" (286).[2]

"Sur la conversion du pécheur"
[On the conversion of the sinner]

This document, amounting to two pages when printed, is dated by Lafuma "with some probability" (290) as belonging to the period, late in 1653, when Pascal began to feel a strong aversion for the "world" and its charms. He evokes eloquently the situation in which the soul, inspired by God, reflects on the nature of the temporal goods to which it (and many others like it) are attached. It sees those goods in a new light, as things perishable, perishing, and indeed already perished. At death the whole order of such things will be withdrawn, and the soul, which is immortal, will remain abandoned and alone. The good truly proportioned to it must be (1) as lasting as the soul, (2) inalienable unless by the soul's consent, and (3) such that nothing is more desirable. Detaching itself from the mass of men, whom it condemns (with humility), the soul starts on a search, rising through the whole range of creatures to the throne of God, their creator. It begins to find its repose in this person who is the supreme and unchanging good, and from whom it cannot be separated except by its own decision. Indeed, to desire God is to possess him ("C'est le posséder que de le désirer, et que le refuser c'est le perdre").[3]

Further reflection obliges the soul to recognize the awful transcendence of God and its own nothingness. Adoration and self-humiliation lead to prayers, appeals to God's mercy, and requests for continuing help. After prayer, action: like a traveler who has lost his way, the soul turns for guidance to those who are more experienced. And so, recognition of the soul's true status includes the following: it is bound (1) as created, to adore its creator; (2) as indebted, to give thanks to its benefactor; (3) as guilty, to make satisfaction to the one it has offended; and (4) as indigent, to pray for further assistance from the one who has shown himself to be the last end.

The fundamental choice among goods, the utter antithesis between creature and creator, the sequence in thought that terminates in a decision to act on the advice of others who are more knowing—all this is quite analogous to the plan of the moral evolution that guides Pascal in composing the opening chapters of the *Pensées*, and it recalls the turn from reasoning to action that emerges at the close of the fragment on the wager.

"Entretien avec M. de Saci" [Conversation with M. de Saci]

The best hypothesis is that this work (of about twelve pages) constitutes a record of several conversations that took place at Port-Royal (early in 1655?) between Pascal and the celebrated spiritual *directeur* and confessor at the convent, Isaac Le Maistre de Saci; and that Saci's secretary, Fontaine, turned Pascal's and Saci's notes into a single dialogue.[4]

(1) Asked by Saci about his readings in philosophy, Pascal gives dense summaries of the opposed doctrines of Epictetus (for whom man is capable of attaining real virtue, of bringing his will into con-

formity with that of God) and of Montaigne (for whom man is uncertain of having any real knowledge, inconstant, and morally weak). These approaches to morality lead to opposed vices: pride and laxity.

(2) Saci admires Pascal's exposé but, in the light of Augustinian principles, he judges such reasonings and subtleties as dangerous for piety. Pascal replies that the positions are compatible with truths from theology: Epictetus sees something of man's dignity before the Fall, Montaigne shows him in his corrupt state. The whole truth requires us to interpret the authors as prefiguring a human nature subject to grace in a way that resembles the union of two natures in Jesus Christ. Taken by themselves the two moralities destroy each other:

car l'un établissant la certitude, l'autre le doute, l'un la grandeur de l'homme, l'autre sa faiblesse, ils ruinent la vérité aussi bien que les faussetés l'un de l'autre. De sorte qu'ils ne peuvent subsister seuls à cause de leurs défauts, ni s'unir à cause de leurs oppositions, et qu'ainsi ils se brisent et s'anéantissent pour faire place à la vérité de l'Evangile. (296)[5]

The Gospel, adds Pascal, reconciles the contradictions by an art truly divine, drawing together what is true and casting out what is false in the two doctrines.

(3) Saci appreciates Pascal's skill—like that of a doctor—in making remedies out of poisons, but still questions the utility of reading such authors. Pascal defends them as useful in troubling complacency; they cannot give virtue, but used against each other they arouse people out of the two main vices to which morality gives rise when taken apart from faith.

The argument of the "Entretien" is, of course, strongly reminiscent of the apologetic project being worked out in the first chapters of the *Pensées*. There Pascal insists on the simultaneous greatness and wretchedness of man as visible in common experience and as repeated in the Stoic and Pyrrhonian schools of philosophy; and there he uses Epictetus and Montaigne as his model figures. However, the resemblance is more than thematic: the "Entretien" shows in a very pure way Pascal's predilection for dialectical reasoning, for posing his problem—in matters of morals and theology—in the form of a far-reaching antithesis that he later resolves by the introduction of a comprehensive third term.

"Abrégé de la vie de Jésus-Christ"
[Abridgment of the life of Jesus Christ]

Of uncertain date (perhaps 1655 or 1656, according to Lafuma),
this work consists of about a dozen pages. It contains first a summary
of the main articles of the Christian faith concerning the things accomplished on earth by God's goodness and through his will, and
especially the Incarnation. According to Pascal men writing from their
own motivation attempted unsuccessfully to set down the events of
this sacred history; then four contemporaries of Jesus Christ, divinely
inspired, wrote their separate accounts. Using and citing verses from
those Gospels, Pascal reconstructs in chronological order the events
in the life of Christ. The result is a series of 354 numbered items of
widely varying lengths (some are phrases rather than clauses or sentences). Occasionally Pascal adds explanatory comments, referring in
some instances to other books of the Bible and to works of St. Augustine, St. Jerome, and others. The narrative begins with the angel
Gabriel's announcement to Zachariah of the birth of John and ends
with an evocation of the last judgment and the eternal union ·of the
elect with Jesus Christ and of Jesus Christ with God. The role of
Christ in this unified biographical *montage* supplements his role in
the *Pensées*, where he is above all the fulfilment of prophecy and
the leading principle in the interpretation of Scripture.

"Ecrits sur la grâce" [Writings on Grace]

These texts (totaling fifteen in number and thirty-seven pages in the
Lafuma edition) are taken from copies of the lost originals, which
were never completed. The grouping and order of printing varies according to the judgment of editors. In Lafuma's opinion they date
from the period 1657–58.[6]

The arguments presented in these "Ecrits" are closely reasoned and
often repetitive from one text to another. Here we have Pascal's most
technical reflections on the ways of God to man. He bases his positions on passages from the Bible, from the works of St. Augustine
and his disciples, from decisions made at the Council of Trent, and
from statements of contemporary theologians. He insists on the distinction between the original state of man after creation and the
fallen state. The change wrought by Adam from the former to
the latter entailed changes in the powers and will of man and in the

will of God as regards the salvation of man. Pascal sums up his case in two admirably constructed sentences. Here is his conclusion: "Concluons donc de ces décisions toutes saintes: que Dieu par sa miséricorde donne quand il lui plaît, aux justes, le pouvoir plein et parfait d'accomplir les préceptes, et qu'il ne le donne pas toujours, par un jugement juste quoique caché" (348).[7] Here is how he applies that conclusion to the great theological debate of his time. (It should be kept in mind that under "Pelagians" he means to include the Jesuits):

> Apprenons par cette doctrine si pure à défendre tout ensemble la puissance de la nature contre les Luthériens, et l'impuissance de la nature contre les Pélagiens; la force de la grâce contre les Luthériens, et la nécessité de la grâce contre les Pélagiens, sans ruiner le libre arbitre par la grâce, comme les Luthériens, et sans ruiner la grâce par le libre arbitre, comme les Pélagiens. (348)[8]

He adds, finally, that we must not think it will suffice to avoid only one of these errors to attain the truth.

The analyses set down in these texts take up the notions of efficacious grace, sufficient grace, and proximate power that are fundamental in the *Provinciales.* They are relevant to the general theme, in the *Pensées*, of divine inspiration as the source of faith, of the search for faith, and of all authentic spiritual life. They also throw light on Pascal's approach to the problem of ambiguous and figurative language in the Bible and in his theological works. With reference to human nature, one notes the analogy between the *misère/grandeur* opposition in the *Pensées* and that of the two heretical views reported here. Moreover, in the final triadic formulation of the problems of grace and free will—with the Lutherans versus the Pelagians and with St. Augustine as the provider of reconciling principles—Pascal applies once again one of his favorite logical devices.

"De l'Esprit géométrique" [On the geometrical mind]

There are two fragments here (about eleven pages in all), the first perhaps conceived as the preface to a geometry textbook for the Port-Royal schools, though clearly not in finished form; and the second perhaps related to the Port-Royal *Art de penser* (*Art of Thinking*, more commonly known in English as the *Port-Royal Logic*). They may be dated no later than 1657–58 (Lafuma).

(1) The first text sets out to explain the method for demonstrating

(as opposed to discovering or discerning) truth, and does so by proposing the model of geometry and its "spirit" or "mind-set" ("esprit"). Geometry is chosen because it defines terms wherever possible, states axioms or self-evident truths, proves propositions that need to be proved, and disposes them in the best order. The discussion of method slips into a treatment of the subject matter of geometry as Pascal understands it: time, space, and number, all of which are interrelated. For they receive a common property: the two infinites; that is, any movement, time, space, or number is relative to a larger or smaller, a longer or shorter, standing thus as a middle term between the two infinites. As a being placed in nature man finds himself involved in this order of extension, number, movement, and time; and he is humbled by it:

Mais ceux qui verront clairement ces vérités pourront admirer la grandeur et la puissance de la nature dans cette double infinité qui nous environne de toutes parts, et apprendre par cette considération merveilleuse à se connaître eux-mêmes, en se regardant placés entre une infinité et un néant d'étendue, entre une infinité et un néant de nombre, entre une infinité et un néant de mouvement, entre une infinité et un néant de temps. Sur quoi on peut apprendre à s'estimer à son juste prix, et former des réflexions qui valent mieux que tout le reste de la géométrie même. (354–55)[9]

(2) The second text, entitled "De l'art de persuader" [On the art of persuading], opens with a consideration of the way in which assent occurs (via the understanding or via the will). If the person addressed believes or desires something that all men believe or desire, that belief or desire takes on the force of an axiom; and if the point at issue is related to that belief or object, one can begin the process of persuasion. The technique is the same as that recommended in the first text, but Pascal now becomes more specific, giving three rules for definitions, two for axioms, and three for propositions. All these may be reduced to two: define all terms, prove everything. This method, Pascal thinks, replaces the useless complications of traditional logic; and since persuasion is assimilated to demonstration, it replaces traditional rhetoric as well.

"De l'Esprit géométrique" repays close reading. These two pieces throw much light on the Pascalian theme of the "disproportion" of man in nature and on a basic drive in Pascal's thought: to engage where possible in discourse that is geometrical either in a literal way or in spirit.

"Comparaison des chrétiens des premiers temps avec ceux d'aujourd'hui" [Comparison of the Christians of early times with those of today]

This text, two and one-half pages long, is divided into fifteen numbered paragraphs. Lafuma dates it as of the period of 1655–57. Pascal judges the Christians of his day to be very inferior to the comsummate Christians of the early church. He traces the cause to the way of entry into the church: then baptism came only after instruction, penitence, knowledge of Christian principles with a lasting commitment in view, a conversion of the heart, and a strong desire for baptism; now, with infant baptism (not condemned in principle by Pascal), the order is reversed and what were the antecedent steps have been forgotten, mainly, it seems, because of negligence on the part of godparents. As a result, the Church is full of people who have not renounced the world and its works. What they must do is submit to receiving the instruction they would have if they were preparing for baptism now.

The *Pensées* show in their apologetic aspect Pascal's prescription for free-thinkers and unbelievers; here he looks at those already in the church and, in effect, sees the need for instruction and discipline like that proposed in the *Pensées*.

"Prière pour demander à Dieu le bon usage des maladies" [Prayer asking God for the right use of illnesses]

The prayer consists of four pages of text divided into paragraphs numbered from 1 to 15. It was composed no earlier than 1659, when a four-year period of illness beset Pascal. He takes his condition as an occasion for an intimate statement of what he thinks his situation as a Christian to be before God, and for an effort to reach a disposition of heart and soul that befits his state. He prays in supremely poignant terms for the moving impulse of grace and for the experience of conversion, with its elements of penitence, redirected affections, and hopes of blessedness. He condemns his past life as having been attached to the world, to its creatures, goods, and pleasures. He believes his present illness to be a punishment for that and a reminder that the order of the world perishes; the only lasting good is God. He asks that his physical suffering and the sadness of his soul may be transfigured so that he may achieve some resemblance to the suffering and sadness of Jesus Christ: then there will be some hope of his becoming lovable in the sight of God. The total and continuous conversion for which he prays points past the regime of nature aided by redemptive grace to the next life and to presence in God's glory.

In this dense and moving document Pascal touches on many familiar themes, coming as close as he can (led on by God; he never wavers on that point) to seeing himself as he believes God must see him, to bringing his will into conformity with what he thinks God's will must be.

"Trois Discours sur la condition des grands" [Three discourses on the condition of men of high rank]

This text of two and one-half pages was published by Nicole in 1670; he claimed to present in it (nine or ten years after the fact) Pascal's ideas and opinions on the indicated subject, which were probably addressed to the young duc de Chevreuse, perhaps in 1660 (Lafuma).

(1) To judge himself and his condition correctly, he must distinguish sharply between his *condition naturelle* or natural status and the status he has by a combination of chance and custom. Although he may act among men according to his rank, he must always remember that he is not superior to them by nature. Simple people do not know this secret; he may decide not to disabuse them, but he should not make improper use of his privileges, nor should he ever be deceived about the character of his title to them.

(2) For a true notion of what obligations others have toward a great gentleman, Pascal works out further the distinction made in the preceding discourse. There are superior qualities ("grandeurs") that are natural and others that are attributed merely on the basis of convention. Respectful external behavior is due the latter; true esteem, which is internal, is reserved for the former. Injustice consists in inverting the two orders of nature and convention, so that one reacts to the first as one should to the second and vice versa.

(3) To understand in turn his obligations to others, the addressee must realize that he controls through position and wealth goods that other men need or desire; he is a "roi de concupiscence" (a "king of concupiscence"). In dealing with others he should be beneficent in

that order (the domain of worldly desires and goods), avoiding the use of force. But this will not take him far; God, the "roi de la charité" (the "king of charity") is his true aim, and lest he lose his soul he must learn to scorn the realm over which he is king.

The contrasting pairs used here—nature/custom, justice/force, concupiscence/charity—serve to link these "Discours" to the analysis of social relationships undertaken by Pascal in the *Pensées*. The insistence on the need to distinguish orders of reality, self-contained but hierarchically related, recalls the great synoptic passage (in fragment 308) on the three *ordres*, two of which—*concupiscence* and *charité* are explicitly evoked here.

"Ecrit sur la signature du formulaire" [Writing on the signing of the formulary]

The original document having been destroyed, this "Ecrit" (amounting to one page of text) consists of passages given in the reply that Nicole composed to what Pascal had written; the date is probably late 1661. In the last of a series of such actions the Assembly of the Clergy ordered on 31 October 1661 the signing of the formulary that condemned the five propositions (see above pp. 17, 21) "in the sense of Jansenius." Pascal set his reflections down apparently with the nuns of Port-Royal in mind.

In his view no distinction can be made between Jansenius's doctrine of efficacious grace and that of St. Augustine and St. Paul. The line of argument previously taken by Arnauld, Nicole, and Pascal himself (see the *Provinciales*, letter 18) held that one could condemn the propositions as heretical (the "question of faith") but deny that they conveyed the doctrine of Jansenius (the "question of fact"). However, that distinction does not appear in any of the official documents, and at this stage in the controversy Pascal thinks it cannot be maintained. He sees three possibilities: (1) to sign without restriction—which condemns Jansenius, St. Augustine, and efficacious grace; (2) to sign with a restriction that excludes the doctrine of Jansenius—which saves both Jansenius and efficacious grace; and (3) to sign as regards faith without explanation or restriction—which is, Pascal declares, a middle way that is useless, unworthy, and abominable. This text was never published, since Pascal decided, after discussion with his friends at Port-Royal, to withdraw completely from the long and bitter dispute, one episode of which had been the composition of that masterpiece, the *Provinciales.*

It is clear that these texts present many difficulties when we try to settle matters having to do with chronology and circumstances of composition; and the fragmentary, unfinished character notable in most of them adds to their elusiveness. And yet—with the exception of the "Discours" on love, which may well be by another author—they assert themselves with indisputable depth and power. They take their places, each with its special line and resonance, in the counterpoint of Pascal's whole oeuvre. They renew our sense of the range of objects to which he turned his attention and of the attitude in which he approached them—with the confidence of a master but with the dedication of a seeker: his intellectual ability and his way with words are deployed not for themselves but for the sake of the hidden truth that waits to be found, proved, or discerned.

Notes and References

Chapter One

1. "As soon as my brother was old enough for one to talk with him, he showed signs of a quite extraordinary mind by the very appropriate little answers he gave, but even more by his questions about the nature of things. This beginning, which aroused high hopes, was never belied afterward, for as he grew older, he grew in reasoning power, so that in that he was far above his physical strength" (Pascal, *Oeuvres complètes, présentation et notes de Louis Lafuma* [Paris, 1963], p. 18). Unless otherwise indicated, all references to page numbers hereafter—both in the text and in the notes—are to this edition.

2. "Anything that is a matter of faith cannot possibly be a matter of reason." Reported in her account of her brother's life. See p. 20 of the edition being used here.

3. See *Oeuvres de Blaise Pascal,* ed. Léon Brunschvicg and Pierre Boutroux (Paris, 1908), vol. 1, p. 210.

4. Pascal's medical history has been the object of considerable investigation and speculation. The best book to consult on the subject is M. Scholtens, *Pascal: Etudes médico-psychologiques* (Assen: Van Gorcum, 1963). It contains summaries in English, French, and German, and a bibliography.

5. "New experiments concerning the vacuum, done in tubes, syringes, bellows and siphons of many lengths and shapes, with various liquids, such as quicksilver, water, wine, oil, air, etc.; with a discourse on the same subject in which it is shown that any vessel, however large one may make it, can be emptied of all elements that are known in nature and that fall under the senses, and what force is necessary to bring about this vacuum" (195).

6. "Light, or rather illumination, is a luminary movement of rays composed of luminous bodies that fill transparent bodies and are moved luminarily only by other luminous bodies" (203).

7. "Total and sweet renunciation ... submission to Jesus Christ and to my spiritual adviser" (from fragment 913 [618]).

8. At the time of Pascal's death at least two copies of his papers were made. The manuscripts and the copies have been the main sources of all subsequent editions of the *Pensées.* Earlier editors favored the manuscripts, and they are indeed irreplaceable, but since about 1950 editors

wishing to reproduce the fragments in the original order have favored one or the other of the copies as the basic text. See below, pp. 118–120.

Chapter Two

1. "But how can a mind like his be awake and not be thinking of something" (26).

2. "It would be easy to justify these two rules and to obtain others. But if I touched on this subject it was because I yielded to the attraction of its novelty. I stop now for fear of tiring the reader by going into too many details."

3. "It is with this problem that I had decided to finish my treatise, not without regret I must say, for I have in my possession many more results; but faced with such abundance, I have made myself set a limit for myself."

4. "It will be easy on that basis for anyone to find the calculations for all these cases, by means of these methods."

5. "There is nothing better known in arithmetic than the proposition according to which any multiple of 9 is composed of figures whose sum is itself a multiple of 9. If, for example, one adds the figures in 18, the double of 9, one finds: $1 + 8 = 9$."

6. "Thus 1719 is a multiple of 9, because the sum—$1 + 7 + 1 + 9$ or 18—of all its figures is itself divisible by 9" (84).

7. "Although the rule is commonly used, I do not think that anyone until now has given a demonstration of it or sought to generalize the principle of it."

8. "I shall set forth also a general method that allows one to determine, by the simple inspection of the sum of its figures, whether a number is divisible by any other number."

9. "[T]his method not only applies to our decimal system of numbering (a system that is based on a convention—a rather unfortunate one, by the way—and not on a natural necessity, as common people think), but also applies without exception to any number system having as its base any number that one may wish."

10. "One may obtain from the foregoing many other propositions that I am omitting, because anyone can easily derive them, and those who may wish to occupy themselves with them will find perhaps some that are more beautiful than those that I might give."

11. "After giving the proportions that are found between the cells and rows of arithmetical triangles, I shall go on to the various applications of those triangles that have 1 as their generator."

12. "But I leave out many more than I give: it is a strange thing how fruitful it [the triangle] is in properties" (54).

13. The letter written by Leibniz is reproduced on pp. 37–38 of the edition used here.

14. "Consequently a plane of infinite extent in any given position necessarily meets a conic surface in any given position."

15. "After those three lemmas and some consequences following from them, we shall give the complete elements of conic sections, namely, all the properties of the diameters, the straight sides, the tangents, etc., and almost the reconstruction of the cone from the data, the description of the sections of the cone by points, etc."

16. "[S]ome beautiful properties, conceived in universal terms, pertaining to the proportions of straight lines drawn to the conic section; and from that follows all that one can say concerning the ordinates" (37).

17. "[T]he fruit of the doctrine of conic sections" (37).

18. "[T]he path traced in the air by a nail on [the circumference of] a wheel as it rolls with its ordinary movement" (117).

19. "It is clear that one finds the whole *roulette* curve in its generating circle alone" (167).

20. "I shall not limit myself to giving you the calculations—of which here is the one for the case I had proposed.... But I shall set forth for you in addition my general method for centers of gravity, which will please you all the more since it is more universal; for it serves equally for finding the centers of gravity of planes, solids, curved surfaces, and curved lines."

21. "Sir, as I learned that M. de Carcavi was to send you some problems that I had proposed concerning the *roulette*, I asked him to add to them the measurement of the curves of all sorts of *roulettes*.... I have only one method for measuring the lines of all sorts of *roulettes*; so that, whether they are simple, elongated or shortened, my construction is always the same."

22. "About four years ago in Italy it was found that a glass tube, four feet long, one end of which is open and the other hermetically sealed, being filled with quicksilver and then having its opening stopped with the finger or in some other way and the tube having been set up perpendicular to the horizon with the stopped opening downward and immersed by two or three finger-breadths in other quicksilver contained in a vessel half full of quicksilver and the other half with water; if one unstops the opening that stands in the quicksilver of the vessel, the quicksilver in the tube descends part of the way, leaving at the top of the tube an apparently empty space, while the bottom of the same tube remains full of the same quicksilver."

23. "[A]llow me to refer you to a universal rule, which applies to all particular cases where it is a question of recognizing the truth" (201).

24. "[I]t is that one must never make a decisive judgment in the negative or in the affirmative of a proposition, unless what one affirms or denies fulfills one of these two conditions: namely, either it appears so clearly and distinctly in itself to the senses and the reason, according as it is subject to one or the other, that the mind has no means of doubting its certainty, and that is what we call *principles* or *axioms*, as, for example, if equals are added to equals, the sums are equal...."

25. "[O]r that it be deduced by infallible and necessary consequences from such principles or axioms, on the certainty of which depends all the certainty of the consequences derived from it; such as this proposition, *the three angles of a triangle are equal to two right angles*, which, not being obvious in itself, is demonstrated clearly and unmistakably by infallible consequences derived from such axioms. Whatever fulfills one of these conditions is certain and true, and whatever fulfills neither is doubtful and uncertain...."

26. "And we reserve for the mysteries of the faith, which the Holy Spirit himself has revealed, that submission of the mind that leads our belief to mysteries hidden from the senses and from reason."

27. "For, as one and the same cause may produce several different effects, a single effect may be produced by several different causes. Thus it is that when one discourses in human terms about the movement [or] the stability of the earth, all the movements and retrogradations of the planets follow perfectly from the hypotheses of Ptolemy, Tycho, Copernicus and from many others that one may invent, only one of which can be true. But who will dare make such a discrimination, and who—without danger of error—will be able to uphold one of them to the detriment of the others?"

28. "You see thereby that even though from your hypotheses all the phenomena of my experiments might follow, it would be of the same nature as the others; and that, remaining always in the terms of probability, it would never arrive at those of demonstration. But I hope to show you one day at greater length that from affirming it [your hypothesis] there follow absolutely things contrary to the experiments."

29. "The universal consent of peoples and the multitude of philosophers are united in the establishment of this principle, that nature would allow its own destruction rather than permit any empty space" (225).

30. "The respect shown to antiquity being today at such a point, in matters where it should have less force, that oracles are made out of all its thoughts, and mysteries even out of its obscurities; that one can no longer propose new things without peril; and that the text of an author suffices to destroy the strongest reasons."

31. "So that the whole succession of men, throughout all the centuries,

ought to be considered as one and the same man who is still subsisting and is continually learning: whence one sees how unjustly we respect antiquity in its philosophers; for, old age being the time most distant from infancy, who does not see that old age in that universal man should not be sought in the times near his birth, but in those that are furthest from them? . . ."

32. "One must consider that some [subject matters] are dependent solely on memory and are purely historical, having as their end only to know what authors have written; the others are dependent solely on reasoning, and are entirely dogmatic, having as their end to seek and discover hidden truths."

33. "But where that authority has its principal force is in theology, because there it is inseparable from the truth, truth which we know only by that authority: so that to give entire certainty in the matters most incomprehensible to reason, it suffices to point them out in the Scriptures (as, in order to show the uncertainty of the most probable things, one need only point out that they are not included therein). . . ."

Chapter Three

1. The English equivalents of these theological terms are: "proximate power," and "sufficient grace." "Grâce efficace," which appears immediately below is "efficacious grace." "Sufficient grace," though adequate, is not always followed by its proper result; one may question whether it provides all that is needed (the "proximate power") for right action. "Efficacious grace," as Pascal conceives it, is always effective. For further details on the subject of grace and the many divisions that have been made in it, see *New Catholic Encyclopedia* (New York: McGraw-Hill, 1967), vol. 6, especially pp. 678–79, 682–83; and also, with special reference to Pascal, J. Miel, *Pascal and Theology* (Baltimore, 1969).

2. "It is permissible for the natural appetite to have the enjoyment of the actions that are proper to it" (410).

3. "Behold, Adam has become like one of us" (Gen. 3:22).

4. "[I]t is impossible that this surprise should not cause us to laugh, for nothing inclines us so much to do so as a surprising disproportion between what one expects and what one sees" (200).

5. "Do you not agree, fathers, that this passage fits our subject perfectly? The letters that I have composed so far are only a game before a real combat. Until now I have only been playing, and showing you the wounds one may inflict on you rather than any I have caused you."

6. "It is a strange and long war when violence tries to oppress truth. All the efforts of violence are unable to weaken the truth, and merely

serve to enhance it further. All the light of truth can do nothing to stop violence, and serves merely to irritate it still more."

7. "Woe to him who is double in heart and who walks in two ways."

8. " 'It is permissible,' say Lessius, Molina, Escobar, Reginaldus, Filiutius, Baldellus, and other Jesuits, 'to kill one who intends to give you a slap on the cheek.' Is that the language of Jesus Christ? Answer us further. Would one be without honor if one suffered a slap without killing the one who gave it? 'Is it not true,' says Escobar, that as long as 'a man allows to live one who has given him a slap, he remains without honor?' Yes, fathers, without that honor that the devil transmitted from his proud spirit into that of his proud children."

9. "To wound a member of your society is to wound the honor of the church" (441).

10. "I have made this one [this letter] longer only because I did not have time to make it shorter" (453).

11. "[E]vil destroys itself by its own evilness" (453).

12. "But Jesus Christ, in whom they [the nuns of Port-Royal] are hidden only to appear one day with him, listens to you and answers for them. One hears it today, that holy and terrible voice, confounding nature and consoling the church."

13. "I have taken it upon myself—I who am in no way involved in that insult—to make you blush in the face of the whole church, so as to bring about in you that salutary confusion of which Scripture speaks, which is almost the only remedy for a hardening such as yours: 'Cover their faces with shame, and let them seek thy name, O Lord' " (Ps. 83:16).

14. "But you have merely changed their heresy according to the occasion. For, as soon as they defended themselves against one, your fathers would substitute another for it, in order that they should never be free from heresy. Thus in 1653 their heresy turned on the quality of the propositions. After that it bore on the *word-for-word*. Later you placed it in the heart. But today no one speaks of that any more; and the intention is that they be heretics unless they sign that the sense of Jansenius's doctrine is contained in the sense of those five propositions."

15. "[S]o admirable is the direction of God in causing all things to work together for the glory of his truth" (463).

16. "[F]or they are without error on the points of faith, Catholic in matters of substance [droit], reasonable in matters of fact, and innocent in both."

17. "I see them nevertheless being so religious in keeping silent that I fear there may be in that some excess" (468).

18. "Leave the church in peace; and I will gladly leave you in peace" (468).

19. "Writings of the Parish Priests of Paris."

Chapter Four

1. "Thoughts of M. Pascal on religion and on some other subjects."

2. The description that follows, which sums up what is now generally agreed to be the case, is based on an enormous amount of work done by generations of editors, but especially on the findings and hypotheses of Tourneur, Lafuma, Mesnard, and Sellier. Readers interested in the history of the editions, the vicissitudes of the original manuscripts that are preserved in the so-called "Recueil original," and the emergence of the two "Copies" as the best base-texts for editions are referred to the masterly introductory pages (13–50) of Jean Mesnard's *Les Pensées de Pascal* (Paris, 1976). See also, in the same volume, appendixes 1–2 (pp. 361–70). Readers of this volume may wish, before going on in chapter 4, to look at pp. 118–120 below, where I give an account of the way in which recent editors have transformed the bases of Pascal studies.

3. "Man's condition: inconstancy, chagrin, anxiety" (503).

4. "True on this side of the Pyrenees, false on the other" (507; fr. 60).

5. "What kind of chimera is man then? How novel, how monstrous, how chaotic, how contradictory, how prodigious? Judge of all things, feeble earthworm, repository of truth, sink of uncertainty and error, glory and refuse of the universe."

These lines sum up one whole side of Pascal's case.

6. "If there is a God, he is infinitely incomprehensible, since—as he has no parts or limits—he bears no relation to us. We are therefore incapable of knowing what he is or whether he is."

7. "And thus our argument has infinite weight, in a game where what is risked is finite, where the chances of winning or losing are even, and where there is an infinite prize to be won" (55; fr. 418).

8. "Proofs. 1. The Christian religion, by its establishment, established by itself so strongly and so gently, while being so contrary to nature. 2. The holiness, elevation, and humility of a Christian soul. 3. The marvels of Holy Scripture. 4. Jesus Christ in particular. 5. The apostles in particular. 6. Moses and the prophets in particular. 7. The Jewish people. 8. Prophecies. 9. Perpetuity: no [other] religion has perpetuity. 10. Doctrine, which explains everything. 11. The holiness of this law. 12. By the order of the world."

9. "There is no doubt that after this, considering the nature of life and the nature of this religion, we ought not to refuse to follow the inclination to follow it, if that inclination comes into our hearts; and it is certain that there is no reason to be scornful of those who do follow it."

10. "Proofs of religion. Morality. / Doctrine. / Miracles. / Prophecies. Figures."

11. "The heart has its reasons of which reason knows nothing" (552; fr. 423).

12. "Submission and use of reason: in that consists true Christianity" (523; fr. 167).

13. "The finite is reduced to nothing in the presence of the infinite" (550; fr. 418).

14. "The infinite distance from bodies to minds shows by analogy the infinitely more infinite distance from minds to charity, for charity is supernatural" (540; fr. 308).

15. "You would not seek me if you had not already found me" (620; fr. 919).

16. "God perceptible to the heart; it is the heart that perceives God and not reason."

17. "Jesus Christ, Saint Paul have the order of charity, not that of the mind, because they wished to warm our hearts, not to instruct. The same with Saint Augustine. That order consists mainly in digression upon each point that is related to the end, so as to keep it [the end] always in sight."

18. See especially the line of reasoning laid down by Lucien Goldmann in *Le Dieu caché: Etude sur la vision tragique dans les Pensées de Pascal et dans le théâtre de Racine* (Paris, Gallimard, 1955), chap. 9, "Le Paradoxe et le fragment," pp. 216–27.

19. "I have not neglected anything."

Chapter Five

1. Chapter 5 presents a revised and expanded version of views expressed in "Le pluralisme méthodologique chez Pascal," which appeared in *Méthodes chez Pascal* (Paris: Presses universitaires de France, 1979), pp. 13–26.

2. "Constant shifting from pro to con" (571; fr. 93).

3. "There are three ways to belief: reason, custom (or habit), inspiration" (603; fr. 808).

4. "Pyrr. [probably = Pyrrhonianism = Skepticism]
"I shall write down my thoughts here without any order, and not perhaps in an aimless confusion. This is the true order, and it will always show my aim by its very disorder."

Chapter Six

1. Among the sources from which I have drawn material for this section I should like to mention especially D. M. Eastwood, *The Revival of Pascal* (Oxford: Clarendon Press, 1936); *Pascal*, ed. A. Lanavère (Paris: Didier, 1969); Gilberte Ronnet, *Pascal et l'homme moderne* (Paris: Nizet, 1963). See also the texts at the ends of the *Provinciales* and the *Pensées*

as edited by Philippe Sellier and Robert Barrault, respectively (Paris: Larousse, 1970, 1965).

Chapter Seven

1. On the question of attribution, see Georges Brunet, *Un Prétendu traité de Pascal: Le discours sur les passions de l'amour* (Paris: Editions de minuit, 1959).

2. "How happy a life is when it begins with love and ends with ambition!" (285). "Man was born for pleasure: he feels it to be so, there is no need for further proof. He follows therefore his reason in giving himself over to pleasure" (286).

3. "To desire him is to possess him, and to refuse him is to lose him" (291).

4. For a thorough discussion of the manner in which the *Entretien* was probably composed, see Pierre Courcelle, *L'Entretien de Pascal et Saci* (Paris: J. Vrin, 1960).

5. "For as one establishes certainty and the other doubt, one the greatness of man and the other his weakness, they destroy each other's truth as well as each other's errors. So that they cannot subsist alone because of their flaws nor unite because of their oppositions, and thus they break and annihilate each other, to make way for the truth of the Gospel."

6. The question is far from settled. For an excellent discussion of the dating of the *Ecrits sur la grâce*, see the "Note on the Date of the *Ecrits*," in Miel, *Pascal and Theology*, pp. 195–201.

7. "Let us conclude then from these very holy decisions [of the Council of Trent]: that God by his mercy gives, when it so pleases him, to the righteous the full and perfect power of fulfilling his commandments, and that he does not give it always, by a judgment that is just though hidden."

8. "Let us learn from this very pure doctrine how to defend at one and the same time the power of nature against the Lutherans and the impotence of nature against the Pelagians; the force of grace against the Lutherans and the necessity of grace against the Pelagians; without destroying free will by grace, like the Lutherans, and without destroying grace by free will, like the Pelagians."

9. "Those who see clearly these truths are able to admire the grandeur and power of nature in that double infinity that surrounds us on all sides, and to learn by that marvelous consideration to know themselves, seeing themselves placed between an infinity and a *néant* ("nothingness") of extension, between an infinity and a *néant* of number, between an infinity and a *néant* of movement, between an infinity and a *néant* of time. Thus one can learn to appreciate oneself at one's true value, and engage in reflections that are worth more than all the rest of geometry."

Selected Bibliography

PRIMARY SOURCES

1. Collected works and other editions

Oeuvres complètes. Edited by L. Brunschvicg et al. 14 vols. Grands
écrivains de la France. Paris: Hachette, 1904–14. Contains texts,
commentaries, contemporary documents related to Pascal. Work of
monumental scholarship. The *Pensées* put into a logical order by
Brunschvicg.

Oeuvres complètes. Edited by J. Chevalier. Bibliothèque de la Pléiade.
Paris: Gallimard, 1954. Readable one-volume edition; introductory
materials, notes. The *Pensées* ordered according to the plan proposed
by Filleau de la Chaise, whose *Discours sur les Pensées de M. Pascal*
(1672) is reproduced in the notes.

Oeuvres complètes. Edited by L. Lafuma. L'Intégrale. Paris: Editions du
Seuil, 1963. Typographically speaking, less readable than the Chevalier edition, but more up to date. The *Pensées* presented in the order
of the first copy of the manuscripts. The edition to which all references in this book apply.

Oeuvres complètes. Edited by J. Mesnard. 2 vols. Bibliothèque européenne.
Bruges: Desclée de Brouwer, 1964–1970. Further volumes planned.
Vol. 1, after 400 pages of historical and bibliographical introduction, presents contemporary documents concerning Pascal; vol. 2
contains works for period 1623–54, with related documents, introductions, notes. Already a great achievement, this edition is replacing
the Brunschvicg edition as the scholarly standard.

Le manuscrit des Pensées de Pascal: reproduction typographique. Edited
by L. Lafuma. Paris: Les libraires associés, 1962. Difficult to find
outside of large libraries, but gives an accurate idea of the *Pensées*
in their extraordinary manuscript form.

Pensées sur la religion et quelques autres sujets. Edited by L. Lafuma.
3 vols. Paris: Editions du Luxembourg, 1951. Vol. 1 contains the
Pensées, in the order of the first copy; vol. 2, notes on each fragment; vol. 3, biographical and other documents, tables of concordance
with principal editions of the *Pensées* for cross-reference from one
edition to another.

Pensées. Edited by P. Sellier. Paris: Mercure de France, 1976. Important
new initiative: follows order of second copy as more faithful than

the first copy to Pascal's intentions. Valuable reconstruction of the chronological framework within which the fragments were apparently composed and classified. Helpful notes, glossary, concordance table of editions, index.

Les Provinciales ou lettres écrites par Louis de Montalte à un provincial de ses amis et aux RR. PP. Jésuites. Edited by L. Cognet. Paris: Garnier, 1965. Excellent introduction places *Provinciales* in historical and theological context. Contains also some related documents, including the *Ecrits des curés de Paris.* Thoroughly annotated.

2. English translations

Pascal. In *Great Books of the Western World,* vol. 33. Edited by R. M. Hutchins and M. J. Adler. Chicago: Encyclopaedia Britannica Inc., 1952. Contains a biographical note, *The Provincial Letters,* translated by Thomas M'Crie; the *Pensées,* translated by W. F. Trotter (using the Brunschvicg order of the fragments); and scientific writings on the vacuum, the equilibrium of liquids, the arithmetical triangle, the theory of probabilities, and, on geometrical demonstration (this last a translation of *De l'esprit géométrique*), translated by Richard Scofield. Quite a lot of Pascal in one volume and in English.

Pensées. Translated by A. J. Krailsheimer. London: Penguin Books, 1966. Recommended. Follows the order and numbering of the Lafuma editions listed above.

Pensées. Translated by W. F. Trotter and edited by H. S. and E. B. Thayer. New York: Washington Square Press, 1965. Follows order of Brunschvicg edition.

Pensées. Translated by John Warrington, introduction by L. Lafuma. London: Dent; New York: Dutton, 1960. Based on an edition by Lafuma in which he redistributed the later fragments of the first copy under headings provided in the earlier chapters of that copy.

Pensées. Translated by H. F. Stewart. New York: Pantheon Books, 1950. Regroups the texts under headings "The Apology" and "Adversaria." French on left-hand page, English facing. Notes and index.

Pensées [and] *The Provincial Letters.* Translated by W. F. Trotter and Thomas M'Crie. New York: Modern Library, 1941. The *Pensées* given in the Brunschvicg order.

The Physical Treatises of Pascal: The Equilibrium of Liquids and the Weight of the Mass of the Air. Translated by J. H. B. and A. G. H. Spiers, introduction and notes by F. Barry, 1937. Reprint. New York: Octagon Books, 1969. Useful translation of works among those less available in English.

Great Shorter Works of Pascal. Translated, with introduction, by E. Cailliet and John C. Blankenagel. Philadelphia: Westminster Press, 1948.

Includes letters as well as the *opuscules*; introductory material on each work.

SECONDARY SOURCES

1. General Works of Biography and Criticism
A. French
Album Pascal. Iconography assembled and commented on by Bernard Dorival. Bibliothèque de la Pléiade, album no. 16. Paris: Gallimard, 1978. Biographical essay in French, with running series of illustrations (350 in all, some drawn from eighteenth, nineteenth, and twentieth centuries). Much authentic food for the imaginations of modern readers of Pascal.

Pascal par lui-même: images et textes. Edited by A. Béguin. Paris: Editions du Seuil, 1967. Introductory essay, extracts, chronology. Illustrated. Recommended.

Croquette, B. *Pascal et Montaigne: étude des réminiscences des Essais dans l'oeuvre de Pascal*. Geneva: Droz, 1974. Important subject, well treated: Pascal's reading and use of Montaigne.

Leroy, G. *Pascal: savant et croyant*. Paris: Presses universitaires de France, 1957. Valuable integrative study.

Mesnard, J. *Pascal*. Les écrivains devant Dieu. Bruges: Desclée de Brouwer, 1965. Pascal and God. Excellent introductory essay, extracts.

Mesnard, J. *Pascal*. Connaissance des lettres. Paris: Hatier, 1967. Highly recommended.

B. English
Broome, J. H. *Pascal*. London: Arnold, 1965. Good general study; treats all aspects of Pascal's life and works.

Mesnard, J. *Pascal*. Translated by Claude and Marcia Abraham. University, Alabama: University of Alabama Press, 1969. A translation of the 1965 item shown above.

Miel, J. *Pascal and Theology*. Baltimore: Johns Hopkins University Press, 1969. Recommended for understanding the background of Pascal's views on grace and human freedom.

Mortimer, E. *Blaise Pascal: The Life and Work of a Realist*. London: Methuen, 1959. Stresses individuality of Pascal and the permanent interest of his work.

Nelson, R. J. *Pascal: Adversary and Advocate*. Cambridge, Mass.: Harvard University Press, 1981. Comprehensive study—biographical, psychological, critical—of Pascal and his works.

Steinmann, Jean. *Pascal*. Translated by Martin Turnell. New York: Harcourt, Brace and World, 1966. Sympathetic, balanced view of the man and the works.

2. Studies of Ideas, Sources, Style, Influences
A. French
Demorest, J. *Dans Pascal: essai en partant de son style*. Paris: Editions de minuit, 1953. Stimulating study of Pascal's literary art.
Gounelle, A. *La Bible selon Pascal*. Paris: Presses universitaires de France, 1970. Brief but clear, penetrating.
Le Guern, M. *Pascal et Descartes*. Paris: Nizet, 1971. Useful investigation of this complex relationship.
Morot-Sir, E. *La Métaphysique de Pascal*. Paris: Presses universitaires de France, 1973. Illuminating study of Pascal's conceptions of language, rhetoric, and metaphysics.
Sellier, P. *Pascal et la liturgie*. Paris: Presses universitaires de France, 1966. Liturgy as an important source of biblical themes and texts for Pascal.
Sellier, P. *Pascal et Saint Augustin*. Indispensable study of a major source and influence.

B. English
Baird, A. W. S. *Studies in Pascal's Ethics*. The Hague: M. Nijhoff, 1975. Judicious discussion of the three "orders" and their ethical consequences.
Topliss, P. *The Rhetoric of Pascal*. Leicester: Leicester University Press, 1966. The *Provinciales* and the *Pensées* as related to classical rhetoric and to seventeenth-century theory and practice. Recommended.

3. On the *Pensées*
A. French
d'Angers, Julien Eymard. *Pascal et ses précurseurs: l'apologétique en France de 1580 à 1670*. Paris: Nouvelles éditions latines, 1954. Detailed account of apologetics in the period indicated and of Pascal's relation to that history.
Harrington, T. H. *Vérité et méthode dans les Pensées*. Paris: Vrin, 1972. "Raison des effets" and other themes studied in a helpful way.
Mesnard, J. *Les Pensées de Pascal*. Paris: S. E. D. E. S., 1976. Comprehensive and authoritative; highly recommended.
Pol. E. *Approches pascaliennes*. Gembloux: Duculot, 1970. Detailed analyses of the twenty-seven titled groups of fragments; at times conjectural but stimulating.

B. English

Davidson, H. M. *The Origins of Certainty: Means and Meanings in Pascal's Pensées*. Chicago: University of Chicago Press, 1979. Studies reason, custom, and inspiration as ways to faith.

Wetsel, David. *L'Ecriture et le reste: The Pensées of Pascal in the Exegetical tradition of Port-Royal*. Columbus: Ohio State University Press, 1981. Excellent study of the relationship between the *Pensées* and Saci's interpretation of the Bible.

4. On the *Provinciales*

A. French

Gouhier, H. "La tragédie des Provinciales." *Table Ronde* 171 (1962): 46–55. Brief treatment of Pascal and the Jansenist-Jesuit quarrel.

Kuentz, P. "Un discours nommé Montalte." *Revue de l'histoire littéraire de France* 71 (1971):195–206. Types of discourse in the *Provinciales*.

B. English

Reisler, M. "Persuasion through Antithesis: An Analysis of the Dominant Structure of Pascal's *Lettres provinciales*." *Romanic Review* 69 (1978)172–85. Substantial study of the framework of Pascal's argument.

Rex, W. Pascal's *Provincial Letters: An Introduction*. London: Hodder and Stoughton, 1977. Reviews historical circumstances of the *Provinciales* and the substance of Pascal's position.

5. On the Mathematical and Physical Treatises

A. French

Costabel, P. et al. *L'Oeuvre scientifique de Pascal*. Paris: Presses universitaires de France, 1965. Best single volume on the subject; at times technical.

Guenancia, P. *Du vide à Dieu: Essai sur la physique de Pascal*. Paris: Maspero, 1976. Close reading of physical works, emphasis on epistemology.

B. English

Baird, A. W. S. "Pascal's Idea of Nature." *Isis* 61 (1970):297–320. Thorough; goes beyond the physical treatises.

"Pascal." In *Dictionary of Scientific Biography*, edited by C. C. Gillispie. New York: Scribners, 1974, 10:330–42. Written by René Taton, the article is clear, authoritative; bibliography at the end.

Index

Works by Pascal referred to in the text are listed under 'Pascal.' Names of Jesuit casuists mentioned in the *Provinciales* are spelled as they appear in the Lafuma edition of the *Oeuvres complètes* (see bibliography).